INTERNAL EVIDENCES OF Christianity

Homer Hailey

Evangelist and Vice President and head of the Department of Bible, Florida College

Charleston, AR:
COBB PUBLISHING
2023

Internal Evidences of Christianity is copyright © 2023 by Cobb Publishing, all rights reserved. This document (whether in whole or in part) may not be reproduced in any way, whether digital, audio, print, or any other means, nor stored in any online system designed for sharing files without prior written permission from the publisher.

Published in the United States of America by:
Cobb Publishing
www.CobbPublishing.com
Editor@CobbPublishing.com
479-747-8372

ISBN: 978-1-960858-87-0

Preface

There is very little being written on evidences today that to this teacher is usable or adequate. That which is written is too often written from the approach of the philosopher or from a philosophical rather than a practical point of view. It could be wished that someone would write a good text from the viewpoint of internal evidence, suitable for freshman and sophomore college level.

Because of this lack of such a text, the materials of this outline were prepared. The material was prepared for sophomore college use; however, the material is so arranged and prepared that it may be adapted to students of any level.

The material is not original, but rather it comprises a compilation of materials, in outline form, from books read by the compiler. Should plagiarism be charged, the charge will be readily admitted; for there was no intention of being original. An effort was made to outline the material as a guide to class discussion, and to outside reading. Outside readings are suggested at the end of most lessons.

It is to be hoped that those who use the outline will find it helpful; and that they will be charitable in the disposition to criticize points that are not as clear to the user as to the compiler. For the outlines were prepared with the objective of any outline only to bring to mind, or to focus attention, on certain points to be elaborated.

Homer Hailey
Temple Terrace, Fla.
September 1, 1963

CONTENTS

INTRODUCTION
1. Proposition and Methodology 8
2. Every Christian — A Defender of the Faith 11

PART ONE — THEISM
3. Introduction to Theism 16
4. Testimony to the Divine Existence 21
5. Additional Evidence for the Divine Existence 25
6. Theism and Revelation 29

PART TWO – THE BIBLE
7. The Bible — Its Profound and Rational Doctrine 34
8. The Unity and Consistency of its Teaching 39
9. The Purity of its Ethics 43
10. Its Relevancy to Human Needs 47
11. The Historical Trustworthiness of the Bible 51
12. Scientific Accuracy of the Bible 55

PART THREE – FULFILLED PROPHECY
13. Israel's History 60
14. The Nations 65
15. Christ in Prophecy 69

PART FOUR – JESUS CHRIST
16. Jesus Christ – "Who Say Ye That I Am?" 74
17. Jesus Christ — The Universal Character 79

18. Jesus Christ — His Moral Glory 83
19. Jesus Christ — The Method and Fullness of His Teaching 87
20. Jesus Christ — The End He Proposed 91
21. Jesus Christ — and Miracles 95
22. Miracles and Their Moral Relationship 103

PART FIVE – THE RESURRECTION

23. "If Christ Be Not Raised" 108
24. His Resurrection — The Witnesses 111
25. The Empty Tomb 117
26. The Witness of Monuments 121
27. Proof From the Conversion of Saul 123

INTRODUCTION

Lesson 1
Proposition and Methodology

This course is designed to acquaint the student of the Bible with an introduction to Christian evidences in general, and especially with the Bible's own internal evidence for the validity of its claim to be a divine revelation. It is sometimes charged that when one uses the Bible to prove its inspiration he is assuming the thing to be proved. The charge is false. Instead, he is investigating and testing the ground of its claims. If one owned *a.* section of land in west Texas and claimed there was oil under it, he would not begin drilling in Louisiana or New Mexico, but he would sink his drill in the middle of the section of land itself. Drilling there would determine the accuracy or falsity of the claim. If one wishes to test the claim of the Scriptures to be the word of God, the Scriptures themselves should be investigated. If, upon investigation, the evidence is sufficiently strong to convince the mind that the Bible is the word of God, the Scriptures themselves should be investigated. If, upon investigation, the evidence is sufficiently strong to convince the mind that the Bible is the word of God, then he cannot but believe. If the evidence is lacking – if "the hole is dry" – then he cannot believe, but must reject it as not being that which has been claimed for it.

It is proposed therefore in this course of study to introduce evidences in general and to investigate and weigh the "internal evidence" itself for the Bible's claim to be the word of God.

DEFINITION OF TERMS
1. Christian Evidence: "Christian Evidence is the scientific proof of the divine authority of the Christian religion" (Keyser). "Christian evidences, as we conceive of it, is especially concerned with

the demonstration of the *factuality* of the Christian religion" (Ramm).
2. Christian Apologetics: "Christian Apologetics is the scientific vindication of the divine authority of the Christian religion" (Keyser). "Christian apologetics is the comprehensive philosophical, theological, and factual demonstration of the truthfulness of our Christian religion" (Ramm).
3. Apology and Apologetics: "These words are derived from the Greek word *apologia (apo* and *logia),* meaning *a discourse in favor of...* In scientific usage these words signify a systematic and closely reasoned vindication." –Keyser, *A System of Christian Evidence,* pp. 21, 22.

PROPOSITION AND PURPOSE OF THE COURSE
1. "Jesus is the Christ, the Son of God."
2. This proposition has much to commend it:
3. It is specific; it is a declaration of facts concerning Jesus.
    a. It is the proposition announced in scripture, Lk. 1:32; Mt. 3:17; Acts 2:36; Acts 2, 3, 8, etc.
    b. It is the proposition declared to be proved in scripture, John 20:30-31. See Everest, *Divine Demonstration,* p. 17-22.
4. "The Bible a Special Divine Revelation."
5. This proposition will become and be the proposition of the course:
    a. It permits a wider range of investigation.
    b. It provides a broader field of evidence and investigation.
    c. It includes all the other proposition includes, while excluding some of the technical studies of the authenticity and credibility of the N.T. books, which study is dealt with in courses in *Introduction.*

Internal Evidences of Christianity　　　10

6. Purpose: To present facts which sustain Christian faith.

METHODOLOGY OF THE COURSE

1. Definition of methodology: "Methodology treats of the scientific way of classifying, correlating and developing the material of any science either as a whole or in any of its branches." Keyser, *op. cit,,* p. 62.
2. The method or procedure to be followed:
   a. Introduction: The Proposition and Definition of terms.
   b. Development of the proposition:
   c. Part One: Theism – Evidence for the existence of God.
   d. Part Two: The Bible – The Evidence of the Book Itself.
   e. Part Three: Prophecy and its Fulfillment.
   f. Part Four: Jesus Christ, the Man.
   g. Part Five: Jesus Christ His Resurrection.

CONCLUSION:

The cumulative nature of the evidence. No one argument by itself will appear conclusive. It is when viewed as a whole that the force of the testimony is appreciated.

References:

H.W. Everest, *The Divine Demonstration,* pp. 9-32.

L.S. Keyser, *A System of Christian Evidence*, pp. 21-23, 62-68.

E.Y. Mullins, *Why Is Christianity True?,* pp. 3-19.

Bernard Ramm, Protestant Christian Evidences, pp. 13-45

Lesson 2
Every Christian a Defender of the Faith

Every Christian should consider himself a "defender of the faith, "able to say with Paul, "I am set for the defense of the gospel" (Phil. 1:17). In order effectively to do this, one must equip himself. This suggests the need for such a course of study in "Christian Evidences."

Such a need is further realized when one considers (1) the doubts which at times arise in his own mind; (2) the contrary teaching to which he or his children are subjected in school, and which he feels he should be able to correct; (3) and the questions presented him by his friends when he discusses the Bible with them.

RATIONAL GROUNDS FOR THE CHRISTIAN AS AN APOLOGIST

1. Human reason is divinely given; it is such that man cannot believe that which seems to him incredible. "We cannot believe unless belief is more rational than unbelief" (Everest, *op. cit,,* p. 13). Therefore, for any belief, the rational ground for that belief must be presented.
2. The powers and functions of reason are limited. Reason must have the necessary evidence before it can decide on the truth or falsity of any proposition. Therefore, reason demands that we have a sufficient and satisfactory ground for our faith in the Word of God.
    a. "But let the evidence be conclusive or demonstrative, and so, also, will be the conclusion... But let their correctness (i.e.,, that of the premises) be conceded, and then Reason has no alternative left but to draw the conclusion and to acquiesce in it, whether she fully comprehends it or not" (Milligan, *Reason and*

Revelation, p. 18).
   b. "To answer this question (Is the Bible of human or divine origin?), on the ground of all evidence variously furnished, is the first province of Reason in matters pertaining to Divine Revelation" *(Idem.).*
   c. "Reason and revelation are not opposed; nor reason and faith. We accept a professed revelation, if at all, because it is reasonable to do so; we put faith in another, and follow him because reason so directs. Reason, or man's intellectual faculties, stands behind everything else." (Everest, *op. cit.,* p. 108).
   d. "Let us remember this fact: Human reason cannot *prove* the Christian religion to be true. It can only show it to be *more reasonable than unbelief"* (Keyser, *op. cit.,* p. 31).
3. The scope of reason: Creation and revelation. One can reason only on that which he finds as a creation, or that which is revealed. (Hamilton, *The Basis of Christian Faith,* p. 25-27).
4. Christian faith is not blind credulity; it rests upon uncontroverted testimony. The Bible warns against being too ready to believe (Mark 4:24; Luke 8:18; 1 John 4:1; 1 These. 5:21).
5. Application of the above reasoning:
   a. The order is: Fact – Evidence – Reason weighs the evidence — deduction or judgment: belief or unbelief.
   b. Acceptance of the evidence depends on five things:
      1) The weight of the evidence.
      2) The clarity with which the evidence is presented.
      3) The honesty of the examiner of the evidence, i.e.,, the hearer.

4) The logical ability of the hearer to evaluate evidence.
   5) The background prejudices of the hearer.

BIBLICAL BASIS FOR THE CHRISTIAN AS AN APOLOGIST

1. God vindicated His ways with men:
   a. The book of Job is such a vindication. In the last section God enters the discussion, vindicates His ways, and closes the debate.
   b. Throughout the book of Isaiah, God called upon Israel to "come reason" with him (Isa. 1:18). God had done great things for Israel; Israel had rebelled; God now decreed the doom of Israel, and the punishment of Judah. But before the punishment He would have them reason with Him and He with them.
2. Jesus Christ defended both His teaching and His conduct: (H.W. Everest, The Divine Demonstration, pp. 9-15. F.E. Hamilton, The Basis of Christian Faith, pp. 15-28. L.S. Keyser, A System of Christian Evidence, pp. 2132. R. Milligan, Reason and Revelation, pp. 15-21.)
   a. He defended His practice when charged by the Pharisees of having cast out demons by the power of Beelzebub (Matt. 12:24-27).
   b. When charged with Sabbath breaking, He made His defense (John 5:19-47).
   c. He vindicated Himself against the charge of "not having learned" (John 7:14-24).
3. Paul's method was to "reason" and "persuade" in "defense" of the faith:
   a. At Thessalonica he "reasoned and alleged" (Acts 17:2).
   b. At Corinth he "reasoned and persuaded" (Acts 18:4).

Internal Evidences of Christianity

    c. At Ephesus he "reasoned with the Jews" (Acts 18:19).
    d. Before Felix it was a matter of "reasoning" (Acts 24:25).
    e. He claimed he was "set for the defense of the Gospel" (Phil. 1:17), and charged Christians to "prove all things" (I Thess. 5:21).
4. Peter exhorted Christians to be ready to give answer (Gk. *apologian)* for the hope within them (I Peter 3:15).
5. Jude urged that all saints "contend earnestly for the faith" once for all delivered (Jude 3).

PART ONE — THEISM

Lesson 3
Introduction to Theism

The Bible makes no formal arguments for the existence of God; it assumes His being. However, it does make allusions to evidence for His existence: The heavens declare His glory, Psalm 19:1-6; Only He can foretell history, Isa. 46:8-11; 48:3; blessings are bestowed from above, Acts 14:17; the cosmos reveals intelligence, Rom. 1:18-22.

In these few lessons the subject can be only introduced. The student is encouraged to prepare himself more thoroughly to meet the wave of infidelity now sweeping the world by study in apologetics and science.

DEFINITION OF TERMS
1. The word "Theism" is derived from the Greek: *Theos,* "God."
2. Christian Theism is the doctrine of God as an imminent, transcendent, personal Being. The Christian defends the doctrine of God revealed in the Bible, not perversions of that doctrine.
3. "Natural Theism is the science which treats of the existence and character of God in the light of nature and reason... The word 'Natural', as used here, should be distinguished thus: its opposite is not 'unnatural,' but 'supernatural.' Christian Theism depends mostly on the supernatural revelation, while Natural Theism depends solely on the light of nature and reason." – L.S. Keyser, *A System of Natural Theism,* p. 11, 12.

THE CONCEPTION OF GOD
1. Its content. "There are variable conceptions of God among the people of earth. They range from the crude, hazy and imperfect ideas of pagan people to

Introduction to Theism

   the clear and correct view that God is the Supreme, Absolute and Infinite Personality who is the First Cause." – *Ibid,* p. 17.
2. Its genesis: whence came the idea, from creation or revelation?
   a. From resident forces in the universe. All explanations for the genesis of the idea of God other than that of revelation must ultimately carry back to the origin from forces resident in matter. But if the idea of God as pure Spirit, infinite in all His attributes and perfections, arose from a pure non-spirit, finite and no-God source, then something came from nothing, which is contrary to all scientific fact.
   b. God revealed Himself. The only alternative to man's development of the idea of God from within, issuing from forces resident in matter, is that of revelation: God revealed Himself to man.
3. Its reasonableness: The majesty of the God of the Bible makes reasonable the existence of such a supernatural Deity who revealed Himself.
   (Hamilton, *op. cit.,* chs. 4, 5)

ARGUMENT FOR REVELATION (A. CAMPBELL)

1. Man has five senses and these are the only avenues through which intelligence concerning material things can reach us.
   a. Only through the sense of smell can one have any idea of odors.
   b. All ideas of savors or tastes must come through the sense of taste.
   c. A person born deaf can have no idea of the nature of sound, and if he develops the art of speaking, it will be in a monotone.
   d. Without sense of sight, one could not have any idea of color, magnitude, or distance.

Internal Evidences of Christianity

   e. Without the sense of touch, one could never originate the idea of material tangibility.
2. Perception — "The mind forms ideas in accordance with the sensations impressed upon the brain. The mind is perfectly conscious of the existence of these impressions; they are communicated directly to the sensorium; and here begins the intellect process of reflecting upon, comparing, and recalling them; then presenting them in different views, separating, abstracting, combining, and generalizing them... Thus it is that we derive our ideas of sensible objects, and thus we begin to reason upon them."
 "The man on whom the light of revelation has never beamed can no more conceive of those ideas which in a system of spiritual religion are native, inherent, and discoverable, than the deaf-born man can be moved by the 'concord of sweet sounds'... We can by things already known be taught things not known; but there must be a teacher."
3. Revelation: "The term revelation, in its strict acceptation among intelligent Christians, means nothing more or less than a Divine communication concerning spiritual and eternal things, a knowledge of which man could never have attained by the exercise of his reason upon material and sensible objects."
4. The intellectual powers of man:
   a. Perception, by which we become acquainted with all things external.
   b. Memory, by which we are enabled to recall all things past.
   c. Consciousness, which acquaints us with all things internal.
   d. The human intellect has no creative power, and the five senses cannot furnish an archetype, a sensation or perception of the spiritual world.

Man can no more create an idea than he can create a material substance or object.
5. Speech is not natural to man but purely imitative. Speech is the result of education.
   a. All philosophers have been baffled in their attempt to account for the origin of language.
   b. Speech, like faith, comes by the ear; whatever comes by the ear is derived; therefore, human language is derived. Whatever is derived is not natural; human language is derived; therefore, human language is not natural.
   c. The idea of anything must necessarily precede the invention of a name for it. There must have been the idea of Deity before the word "God" could have been invented.
      1) The word "steamboat" was not in the vocabularies of the world until the idea had existence. (How about the word "astronaut" in Campbell's day?)
      2) The invention of the terms by which spiritual ideas are expressed must have been posterior to the conception of the ideas. The ideas could not have been derived through the senses, they must have come about in some other way – both the idea and the names of spiritual things must have been by divine revelation.

CONCLUSION:
"Man could not invent, or originate the idea of a God, a Spirit, a future state, or any of the positive institutions of religion; he could never have invented or originated the ideas inseparably connected with the word priest, altar, sacrifice, etc., ergo, that these ideas and the words used to express them, are derivable only from an immediate and direct revelation; man having no power according to any

philosophic analysis of his intellectual powers, to originate any such ideas."

References:
- Charles E. Brown, *Why I Believe in Religion,* Chapter 1.
- A. Campbell, *Campbell-Owen Debate.*
- E.J. Cornell, *A Philosophy of the Christian Religion,* pp. 274-329.
- Clarke, *An Outline of Christian Theology,* pp. 63-102.
- *Fundamentals,* Vol. VI, pp. 22ff; Vol. VIII, pp. 90ff.
- Floyd E. Hamilton, Basis of Christian Faith, Chapters III, IV, V. *International Standard Bible Encyclopedia*, Article: "God."
- L.S. Keyser, *A System of Natural Theism.*
- L.S. Keyser, *A System of Christian Evidence*, pp. 189-191.
- James Orr, *Christian View of God and the World*, pp. 75-111.

Lesson 4
Testimony to the Divine Existence

In this lesson are introduced the "Cosmological" and the "Teleological" arguments. These are defined by Keyser as follows:

"The *Cosmological Argument* is the argument that the cosmos is an effect produced by a Primal Cause, which, from the nature of the case, must be a Person. Sometimes it is called the argument from causality, or from cause and effect." – L.S. Keyser, *A System of Natural Theism,* p. 46.

"The *Teleological Argument* is the argument for the divine existence which is based on the evidence of design, purpose and adaptation in the creation. It is best known as the argument from design, purpose or final cause." *Ibid.,* p. 30.

The two arguments are closely related. The cosmos argues for a cause, and design argues for a designer. Though the arguments are not developed by the apostle, Paul introduces the two as grounds for the Gentiles being "without excuse" for their condition.

GOD'S WITNESS OF HIMSELF
(Romans 1:20. Read also vv. 18-28)
1. The things which are made: the cosmos, universe. In it is seen order, design, intelligence.
2. The invisible things: power and divinity.
   a. Power: that which brought into existence the universe and now controls it.
   b. Divinity: supreme intelligence and will which directed and continues to direct the power.
   c. These are clearly seen through the things made: the cosmos.
3. Diagram of the proposition of Rom. 1:20: Power: *God, Divinity.* "Things" *invisible things, a cosmos, made.* We do not say "everything must have a

Internal Evidences of Christianity

cause," but that every *effect* must have an adequate cause. Hence, we get back to that which is not an effect, but the uncaused cause of all: God.

PRINCIPLES AS BEGINNING POINTS
1. In logic there must be an A and a Z, a point beyond which the mind cannot reason in beginnings, and a point in the future beyond which the mind cannot travel with clarity, a stopping point. The Christian theist begins and ends with God (the beginning, Gen. 1:1; the end, 1 Cor. 15:24-23). The atheist must begin and end with something else – but with what?
2. An unvarying law of logic: Begin with a fact that is universally conceded and reason from that fact to a conclusion. The only concession asked is that it be conceded that the universe is a *cosmos,* not a *chaos.* This should be universally recognized.
3. Another principle with which to begin: "Out of nothing, nothing comes." Something is, therefore something was. A cosmos is, therefore power, intelligence, and will were. (Harry Rimmer, *Harmony of Science and Scriptures)*

FACTORS AND COMBINATIONS IN THE UNIVERSE WHICH DEMAND INTELLIGENCE
(From Rimmer, *op. cit.)*
1. Factors:
   a. In arithmetic: 9 numerals and a naught.
   b. In literature: 26 letters.
   c. In matter: 96 or more elements.
2. Combinations: From combinations of these come mathematical solutions, literature, and the cosmos.
   a. Arithmetic: select the first three, combinations 123, 321, 132, 312.
   b. Literature: select four letters and four combinations, but such difference in ideas: star,

rats, tars, arts.
- c. Matter: diamond, graphite, coal, clay, but all from same elements.
3. How are these combinations formed?
   - a. Chance – try with mathematics, literature, matter.
   - b. Law – but law necessitates a lawgiver. Who is the lawgiver?
   - c. Nature – but what is nature? It is blind force acting without intelligent direction, or it is force directed by intelligence. This brings us back to the problem: If there is sufficient evidence in the cosmos to make it more reasonable to believe that an intelligent will directs than to believe that blind force controls, then one must believe that such a Being as God exists.
   - d. Intelligence – If intelligence directs the combinations then the combination will appeal to intelligence. If intelligence directs the combination of elements that make up the cosmos then we must admit the being of God, for intelligence connotes personality, and that personality is God.

DESIGN IN THE UNIVERSE

(A. Cressy Morrison, *Man Does Not Stand Alone*) The natural order: From the atom to the unfathomable universe the stamp of design is clearly imprinted on all.
1. The planets and the accuracy of "time."
2. Evaporation, precipitation, and the operation of intelligent law. Vegetation, animal, to man. Each is designed for the other, and that for a purpose.
3. Instinct: of spiders, bees, the wasp, dirt-dauber, birds, animals. Whence did it come? It is the product of intelligence, or of unguided force. Can such a cause as blind force produce such an effect?

Internal Evidences of Christianity 24

4. Chemistry and physics: water to ice, to vapor, etc; the combination of chemicals to make air, and its design for such a universe.
5. All of these plus thousands of others argue for a designer, for in all with which we are acquainted there is no design apart from an intelligent designer.

CONCLUSION:

In the midst of a cosmos, with design and intelligence stamped upon every phase of this cosmos, it is more reasonable to conclude there is a designer than to believe any other hypothesis. Design connotes a designer; a designer connotes intelligence; intelligence connotes personality; and this personality we call God.

An effect demands an adequate cause. It is admitted that the cosmos is an effect, the result of the operation of power upon matter. But such an effect demands an adequate cause; and an adequate cause can be found only in an intelligent director of that power. This leads us back to God, the point Paul was making in Romans 1:20.

References:

Edward J. Carnell, *An Introduction to Christian Apologetics*, p. 122-190

Clarke, *An Outline of Christian Theology*, p. 102-128, 128-161

Chas Hodge, *Systematic Theology,* Vol. I, p. 191-240

L.S. Keyser, A System of Christian Evidence, p. 192-194

A Cressy Morrison, *Man Does Not Stand Alone*

E.Y. Mullins, *Why Is Christianity True?*, p. 72-90

Harry Rimmer, *Harmony of Science and Scripture*, p. 11-49

Wilbur Smith, *Therefore Stand, p. 272-358*

Modern Science and Christian Faith, a symposium of writers (Van Kampen Press)

Lesson 5
Additional Evidence for the Divine Existence

In this lesson additional evidence for the existence of a supreme and divine Being can only be introduced. All of these arguments are related to the Teleological and Cosmological Arguments. It is sometimes difficult to determine where one ends and the other begins.

THE GENERAL ARGUMENT
1. Definition: "The General Argument is that form of theistic proof which is based on the universal belief in God and the religious instinct." – L.S. Keyser, *A System of Natural Theism,* p. 24. 2. The universal belief in God.
    a. History and ethnology prove that all nations have a belief in a supernatural Being or in Supernatural beings. The ideas may be crude, but they nevertheless exist.
    b. Either He exists or He does not. If not, then material substance is the only entity, and it has produced the idea. But the idea being false, material substance becomes the universal falsifier.
    c. Apply the law of causality. If God exists, we have an adequate cause for such an effect. If He does not, there is an effect with no adequate cause.
2. The universal religious instinct.
    a. Men in all the world, and throughout all time, not only believe in deity, but also engage in acts of worship and devotion.
    b. The religious principle is extremely potent in all nations, dominating their thought and history.

      c. Everywhere the human heart has a craving for God. There will be exceptions as individuals, but the exceptions do not invalidate the rule.
3. The conclusion would be that as there is that in the universe which satisfies all man's cravings, there must be a reality to complement and answer this universal craving for God.

THE MORAL ARGUMENT

1. Definition: "The Moral Argument is the proof of divine existence which is based on the moral constitution of man and the moral order of the world." – L.S. Keyser, *op. cit.,* p. 60. (This argument is closely related to the Cosmological Argument.)
2. Man possesses a moral nature. As to the origin and nature of conscience there may be debate, but as to its existence there can be none. True joy and happiness come from right being and conduct.
3. The moral order of the world.
    a. The testimony of history: right lauded, wrong short-lived. History vindicates the right and condemns the wicked, even though tardily.
    b. Society and government are based on a moral order.
    c. Natural consequences of right and wrong prove a moral order.
4. A moral economy demands a personal Creator and Governor.
    a. The moral could never have sprung from the non-moral by means of "resident forces," for there could be no such resident forces in a purely non-moral universe.
    b. Moral qualities can be predicated only of persons -hence, a personal author.
    c. Present inequality and injustice demand an

inevitable judgment and a personal Judge of such matters.

THE ESTHETICAL ARGUMENT

1. Definition: 'The Esthetical Argument is the argument for the divine existence which is based on the presence of beauty and sublimity in the universe." – L.S. Keyser, *op. cit.*, p. 72.
2. The fact of beauty:
   a. In nature. In spite of all that may be dreary or monotonous, there is much (most) in the world that is beautiful and lovely.
   b. In the human physique: face and figure. Cf. the distorted with the perfect.
   c. In human art: Art, literature, architecture, music.
3. Man's esthetic faculty responds to the beautiful in nature. Not eye alone, but an inner soul that thrills to and demonstrates capacity for the beautiful.
4. The rational inference:
   a. The evidence of design: "Since so much beauty and grandeur mark the universe, and since man has an innate esthetic taste to match them, the rational conclusion is that the cosmical beauty and man's taste must have been designed to complement each other.. *"op. cit..* p. 24.
   b. Evidence of divine love of the beautiful. Much that is beautiful is unseen and unnoted by men. Why does it exist? It is evidence of the divine love for the beautiful.
   c. The repulsive only accentuates the beautiful and sublime.

CONCLUSION:

It is not claimed that the existence of God can be proved. It is claimed that the evidence which testifies to such a Being is so overwhelming that it is more rational and reasonable to believe than to disbelieve.

References
- Chas. E. Brown, *Why I Believe in Religion,* pp. 1-28.
- Wm. N. Clarke, *The Christian Doctrine of God*, pp. 357-471.
- ----- Clarke, *An Outline of Christian Theology*, pp. 68-161.
- E. Hamilton, *Basis of Christian Faith*, pp. 44-55.
- L.S. Keyser, *A System of Natural Theism*, pp. 24-79.
- Jas. Orr, *Christian View of God and the World*, pp. 75-111.
- Paley, *National Theology*, pp. 9-57.

Lesson 6
Theism and Revelation

The cosmos can only testify that power and will guided by intelligence pervade the universe. The will of that power toward rational creatures had to be revealed. In this lesson it is proposed that the relation between the evidences of nature and the evidences of revelation are so related as to demonstrate that the author of each must be the same Divine Person.

THE INSUFFICIENCY AND THE SUFFICIENCY OF NATURE
1. What nature cannot tell one:
   a. From whence came the individual?
   b. Whither are we going?
   c. What is the purpose of man and of life?
   d. What is the relation of man to his Creator?
   e. What is the character of the creator? moral or non-moral?
   f. Does the Creator love? hate? or without emotions at all?
   g. Is He concerned with mercy or justice? does He combine the two? If there is fellowship between the Creator and the creature, should it be broken can it be restored?
   h. What is absolute right?
   i. What is absolute wrong? or is there no standard of either?
2. In the natural world there is that which supplies and gratifies every need and desire of the physical man: a. Food and water for hunger and thirst (cf. the various kinds of food). b. Everything necessary for good health; but man must find it.
   a. Beauty for the esthetic.
   b. The opposite sex for companionship and

Internal Evidences of Christianity 30

completeness of each.
3. There is no physical appetite or desire but what there is that which gratifies and satisfies it. Yet there is that about man which the physical does not satisfy (Psalm 42:1). This is demonstrated by man's insatiable desire beyond the physical necessities of life. Cf. the millionaire who wants another million.
4. But God, as revealed in the Bible and in the Christ, completely and fully satisfies this spiritual desire. There is not a spiritual hunger or thirst or longing but finds its satisfaction in God. Natural revelation is general: power and divinity. "But that power and divinity stand in no specific relation to the individual." (James Orr, *Revelation and Inspiration*, p. 48.)
5. This completeness and fulness of the physical man in the realm of the natural and physical, and the completeness and fulness of the spiritual in God as revealed, argue for the one author of both. He possessed a full and complete knowledge of man and of his needs, and likewise possessed the power to provide for those needs.

THE ABSOLUTE IMPERATIVENESS FOR A REVELATION

1. The universal knowledge of and belief in deity testifies that such a revelation has been made, Rom. 1:18-21; which revelation was rejected, vv. 22-23.
2. In nature two attributes of God are revealed: *power* and *divinity*. But Himself as Spirit, love and light, and His will to an intelligent being had to be revealed. These He has revealed completely in Jesus Christ, John 14:7-10; 17:3; 2 Cor 5:18-21; Heb. 1:1.
3. Through or by the Holy Spirit these things have now been made known, I Cor. 2:613; Eph. 3:1-6.
4. The inevitable consequence of rejecting that light

which man possessed has been seen in history, past and present, Rom. 1:24-28; Eph. 2:11-12; 4:17-23.

Since God has revealed Himself, both as to power and righteousness, in nature and by revelation, He now commands men that they should all everywhere repent. Repentance becomes God's universal command, Acts 17:30-31.

CONCLUSION:

God's revelation through nature of His power and divinity, and His revelation in Jesus Christ of His character and righteousness and will, leaves man without excuse for his unbelief. The evidence is sufficient to convince every honest man and woman. There is no other adequate explanation for either the cosmos or the Bible.

References:

Lorraine Boettner, *Studies in Theology*, p. 9-49.
James Orr, *I.S.B.E.*, "Revelation."
James Orr, *Revelation and Inspiration*, p. 46-66.
Benjamin B. Warfield, *The Inspiration and Authority of the Bible* (Intro, by Van Til, pp. 668), 71-102, 131-166.

PART TWO – THE BIBLE

Lesson 7
The Bible — Its Profound and Rational Doctrine

The proposition of the course is, "The Bible a Special Divine Revelation." There is need for such a revelation; for although "the heavens declare the glory of God" (Ps. 19:1), the apostle affirms only His "power and divinity" are seen through the things made (Rom. 1:18-21). Therefore, God's nature, character and will to man had to be revealed in a special way. This revelation God has made through His Son, John 1:1-4, 14-18; 7:29; 14:6-10; Heb. 1:1-3; Col. 1:15-18; 2:8-10; and preserved in the inspired word which was revealed by the Holy Spirit, I Cor. 2:1-16.

The proof of such a revelation is cumulative, each argument becoming a part of the whole. The proposition of this particular lesson is, "The profound and rational doctrine of God, man and redemption, as presented in the Scriptures, prove the Bible to be a special divine revelation."

THE BIBLE DOCTRINE OF GOD

The Bible was written by about forty individuals, over a period of more than fifteen hundred years, yet the picture of God is consistent throughout. No contradictory notes are struck. He is presented as personal: He loves, hates, sees, acts, and is constantly mindful of his creation. Such a view is both "profound" and "rational."

To him are ascribed such attributes as follows, which are found from early to late writings:
1. *Eternal* or *self-existence.* His name is "Jehovah, the I AM, the Self-existent One," Ex. 3:13, 14; Isa. 43:10-11; 48:12; John 8:58; Rev. 1:8; 4:8.
2. *Eternity and Omnipresence.* Time and space are conditions of human thought. In our thoughts there

is *A where* and *A when* to everything. For God, the Absolute Being, there are no such limitations, Ps. 90:2 (Moses, ca. 1400 ; Heb. 1:10-12; Ps. 139:7-10; Acts 17:26-28.
3. *Omnipotence.* He is infinite in power: as revealed in creation, Gen. 1:1-2 by direct statement, Gen. 17:1; Isa. 40:12, 26; and in the worship of Him by the angels, Rev. 4:8.
4. *Omniscience.* That He is infinite in Knowledge and wisdom is revealed in His works, in prophecy, and by direct statement, Isa. 46:10; Heb. 4:13, etc.
5. *Infinite in Holiness.* This is perfectly revealed in Jesus Christ, the sinless one. Hatred for sin is manifested from Eden to the Judgement.
6. *Unchangeableness.* The same unchangeableness is revealed in both covenants Num. 23:19; Mal. 3:6; James 1:17.
7. *Merciful, Longsuffering, Compassionate.* He is revealed as being merciful, compassionate, giving man every opportunity to repent and turn to Him, but punishing the guilty always, Gen. 6; 2 Pet. 3:9; 1 Pet. 5:6, 7; Book of Revelation.

THE BIBLE DOCTRINE OF MAN

Here again the Bible is consistent throughout. It never strikes a false note regarding man, nor does it contradict a conception formerly presented. This cannot be said of philosophers or philosophies.
1. From Genesis through Revelation, man is presented as personal, moral, in the image of God, and possessing power to choose between right and wrong.
2. He is presented as triune: "spirit," "soul," "body," I Thes. 5:23; as "inward man" and "outward man," 2 Cor. 4:16.
3. Throughout the Scriptures, God and Satan are

Internal Evidences of Christianity 36

presented as appealing to the will of man.

God appeals to the will by an appeal to the intellect, affections and reverence or godly fear of man. Satan appeals to the will through an appeal to the lust of the flesh, lust of the eye, and the pride of life. See Gen. 3; Matt. 4:1-11; I John 2:15-17. As a moral creature, possessing power to choose, man makes his own choice, thus becoming responsible for his conduct and condition.

THE BIBLE DOCTRINE OF SALVATION

1. Sin is always revealed as rebellion against God. Man is constantly portrayed as unable to save himself. God is always the Saviour.
2. Salvation is always moral, never forced. God invites; man chooses, Isa. 1:18; 65:2; Matt. 11:28-29; 23:37; 2 Cor. 5:11.
3. From beginning to end the Bible unfolds a unified definite plan of salvation: repentance by man, forgiveness by God. God's appeal is ever for inner purity, not for mere external form.
4. From beginning to end there is the altar, sacrifice, priest. The entire plan of human redemption culminates in salvation by a divine sacrifice, worthy of the mind of God.

CONCLUSION:

The Bible's profound and rational doctrine of God, man and salvation takes the book outside the realm of a human production. The consistency of presentation of the theme over such a long period of time is evidence that back of the presentation there is one over-ruling and guiding mind.

References:

H.W. Everest, *Divine Demonstration,* pp. 124-162.

Alfred Earnest Garvie, *Handbook of Christian Apologetics,* pp. 138-185.

Charles Hodge, *Systematic Theology,* pp. 366-441.

L.S. Keyser, *A System of Christian Evidence*, pp. 77-80.
L.S. Keyser, *A System of Natural Theism,* pp. 130-138.
J. Gresham Machen, *Christianity and Rationalism,* pp. 54-68; 69-79.
James Orr, *God's Image in Man,* p. 33-78; 249-283.

Lesson 8
The Unity and Consistency of its Teaching

The arguments now to be presented in support of the proposition, The Bible a Special Divine Revelation, are drawn from the unity and consistency of the Bible's teaching, supplemented by lessons on its historical trustworthiness, soberness, and the all-sidedness of its teaching. A fair and impartial study of the Bible itself becomes one of the best arguments for the proposition affirmed.

UNITY IN STRUCTURE
1. The Bible manifests an architectural plan: *Two testaments,* each in *three parts: historic, didactic, prophetic;* and with each testament looking to *the past, the present,* and *the future.* The whole is made up of 66 books, written by about forty men, over a period of about 1500 years. In these are to be found *variety* and *diversity: History* and *poetry, laws* and *lyrics, prophecy* and *symbol.* Yet they unite to declare one grand theme: God and human redemption.
2. It may be compared to:
   a. Solomon's temple: stones, wood, etc., prepared at the quarry and in the forest, each fitting perfectly when brought together, 1 Kings 6:7.
   b. A great orchestra or symphony, all the parts combining to make one great song.

UNITY IN DOCTRINE, OR UNITY IN ITS MAIN THEME
1. The grand theme of the Bible is *God and Human Redemption.* Throughout it teaches the same consistent doctrine of God, man, morality, sin

salvation and immortality. Not a discordant note.
2. In remedying sin, there is found in every dispensation -Patriarchal, Mosaic, and Christian – three things: *priest, sacrifice, altar.*

UNITY IN PROPHECY – PROPHETY
1. Of all prophecy there is but one center: *the kingdom and the King.* The kingdom is one of *righteousness;* the King is to be *Saviour.*
2. Two great events are prophesied: O. T.: The *King coming* to *redeem* and to *reign;* N. T.: The *King reigning,* but coming to *judge* and to ' *deliver* the kingdom to the Father to consummate God's eternal plan.

UNITY OF TEACHING – ITS DIDACTIC UNITY
1. In not one respect are these doctrinal and ethical teachings in conflict, from beginning in Genesis to end in Revelation. Where some have tried to set the writers at variance investigation proves them a unity, e.g., Paul and James on the doctrine of faith.
2. There is a progressive development of revelation, a progressive unfolding of doctrine throughout. It has been compared to the starlit, moonlit, and sunlit ages.
3. This didactic and progressive unity could not be realized till the book was complete. With the entire Bible in one's hand, he can discover a divine eternal purpose running throughout the book from beginning to end.

ORGANIC UNITY – THE UNITY OF THE BIBLE IS AN ORGANIC UNITY
1. Organic unity implies three things: first, that all parts are necessary to a complete whole; secondly, that all are necessary to complement each other; and thirdly, that all are pervaded by one life-principle.

2. Apply these laws to the Word of God: a. All the parts of the Bible are necessary to its completeness. Organic unity is dependent on the existence and cooperation of organs: the human body as an example. Consider the books of the Bible: Esther, Ruth, Job, Song of Solomon of O. T.; Philemon, Revelation, etc., of the New. Each makes a contribution to the completeness of revelation. b. The second law of organic unity is that all parts are necessary to complement each other. Examples:
3. The Four Gospels. Each has a specific purpose: to Jews, Romans, Gentiles, universal. Beginning: genealogy, majesty, humanity, divinity; close: resurrection, ascension, parting benediction, hint of second coming.
4. The Epistles. Five writers: Paul, faith; Peter, hope; John, love; James, works; Jude, against false teachers.
5. The Decalogue demands the Sermon on the Mount; Isaiah's prophecy demands the narratives of the Gospels; Leviticus the book of Hebrews; the Mosaic code the ethics of the epistles; the first chapters of Genesis the last chapters of Revelation.
6. The third and last law of organic unity is that one life principle must pervade the whole. The life of God is in His word throughout -*God breathed – 2 Tim. 3:16V.*

THE SOBERNESS OF ITS TEACHING
1. The manner of its teaching is calm, simple, dignified. It is neither cold and intellectual nor fanatical and sensational. It presents a simple statement of truths with a warm confidence of the truthfulness of the things said.

THE ALL-SIDEDNESS OF ITS TEACHING
1. Every human system over-stresses some things and

Internal Evidences of Christianity 42

under-stresses others, thus becoming defective. This is not true of the Bible. Consider its teaching on the following subjects.
2. The relation of nature and spirit.
3. God and the world. Cf. pantheism and deism.
4. Man's dual nature, body and soul, without minimizing the value of either, but giving to each its proper importance.
5. Practical life and the mystical communion with God.
6. Present life and future life.

CONCLUSION:

It is more reasonable that such a book is the product of one Divine Mind rather than the product of so many minds over such a long period of time. Keep in mind that the evidence for the proposition is cumulative.

References:
Louis Berkhof, *Principles of Bible Hermeneutics*.
J.D. Bales, *Roots of Unbelief,* (see Index)
George DeHoff, *Why We Believe the Bible*, pp. 102-119.
H.W. Everest, *Divine Demonstration,* pp. 107-254.
B. Franklin, *The Gospel Preacher,* Vol. I, pp. 11-34.
Fundamentals, Vol. VII., pp. 55-69.
Floyd T. Hamilton, *Basis of Christian Faith*, pp. 150-163.
L.S. Keyser, *A System of Christian Evidences*.
B. Ramm, *Protestant Christian Evidences,* pp. 224-249.
Z.T. Sweeney, *N.T. Christianity,* Vol. II., pp. 340-383.

Lesson 9
The Purity of its Ethics

The subject of ethics is usually divided into two classifications: General Ethics and Christian Ethics. These may be defined as follows:

"General Ethics is the science of right and wrong in principle, character and conduct." "Christian Ethics is the science of right and wrong in the light of Christian teaching. Ethics deals specifically and only with the problem of *morality,* of right and wrong." — L.S. Keyser, *A System of Christian Ethics,* pp. 19, 22, 24.

The expression "in principle, character and conduct" would include not only the actions of an individual, but the principle involved in that action, and the thoughts, the very heart of the individual from which the conduct proceeds. A man might conduct himself acceptably according to the general standard of conduct, yet he might not be an ethical man; for "As a man thinketh in his heart, so is he" (Prov. 23:7), and, "Blessed are the pure in heart: for they shall see God" (Matt. 5:8). "Ethics belongs pre-eminently to the inner nature, to the motives, the feelings and the thoughts." — Keyser, *op. cit.,* p. 20. "Everywhere in the Bible clear moral distinctions are drawn; there is no blurring of them, as is the case in the ethnic religions and in most of the schemes of human speculation." Keyser, *A System of Christian Evidence,* p. 80.

IN THE BIBLE RIGHTEOUSNESS IS EVERYWHERE COMMANDED AND COMMENDED: SIN IS ALWAYS CONDEMNED

1. *Creation.* At the completion of creation God pronounced everything, including man, 'Very good" (Gen. 1:31). This included moral and physical creation. From the beginning a distinction was made when the tree of knowledge of good and evil was

put in the midst of the garden (Gen. 2:16, 17).
2. *The flood.* The antediluvians were destroyed because of excessive wickedness (Gen. 6:5), while Noah was saved because. he was a "righteous man" (Gen. 6:9; 7:1).
3. *The Nations.* Nations and peoples were punished and destroyed, but always because of their wickedness. No nation was ever dealt with severely when it walked in the way of righteousness:
   a. *The Amorites,* whose land Jehovah promised to Abraham. He could not give it to him at the time because it could not justly be taken from them. His seed should sojourn in another land, and Abraham should go to his fathers: "And in the fourth generation they shall come hither again: for the iniquity of the Amorite is not yet full" (Gen. 15:16). But when Israel came out of Egypt, God could in all justice and righteousness give to them the land of the Amorites, Lev. 18:24-30; Deut. 9:4, 5.
   b. *Sodom and Gomorrah.* Both were destroyed because of excessive wickedness but could have been spared had there been sufficient righteousness there. When Abraham pled with God for the city on the ground of ten righteous persons God said, "I will not destroy it for the ten's sake" (Gen. 18:20-32).
   c. *Israel and Judah.* These went into Assyrian and Babylonian captivity because of their failure to keep His commandments in righteousness, Deut. 30:15-20.
II. *Specific Teaching* found in the Bible, demanding a high moral standard: a. The Ten Commandments followed by an exceeding high code of laws to be observed by the community, punishing some crimes by death, Exodus 20-23. b. The Psalms, covering

nearly the whole of Israel's history, abound in ethical teaching, Ps. 89:14; 45:6; etc.

III. *The Sermon on the Mount*: this is unsurpassed for ethical grandeur. Matt. 5-7. Not a moral principle has added to the Sermon on the Mount since the day that it was preached by Jesus. Jesus puts the emphasis on the heart, the source of the act.

INNER PURITY – NOT MERELY OUTWARD, CEREMONIAL MORALITY – IS ALWAYS DEMANDED

1. The ritual of sacrifice was given to Israel by Jehovah at the very beginning of her natural history, the object of which was to develop a sense of righteousness in its condemnation of sin. The sacrifices were associated with repentance and forgiveness, the blood being for atonement, Lev. 17:11-14.

   When ritual began to take the place of holiness and righteousness of conduct such was condemned by the prophets, and inner purity demanded even though ritual was the order of all the nations round about Israel. Whence came this higher ethical conception? Isa. 1:14-17; Hosea 6:4-6; Amos 5:21-24; Micah 6:6-8.

2. Throughout, in its teaching the Bible demands inner purity, not mere ritual, Prov. 4:23; Ps. 19:14; 51:1-19; Matt. 5:8; 5:20.

OBJECTIONS

The objector to the Bible's claim to be a special divine revelation will deny that the Bible presents a perfect standard, raising questions concerning:

1. The destruction of ancient cities and nations such as the Amorites and the Amalekites. But to these God had given time to change (Gen. 15:16). They became more corrupt, till unfit to live. This only

sustains our point of the high ethical demands of the God of the Bible.
2. David, of whom God said, "I have found David a man after my heart, who shall do all my will" (Acts 13:22; see also I Samuel 13:14), but who committed adultery and sought to cover it with murder. Let the Bible student remember that God condemned his sin, and that David suffered the consequence of his wrong-doing as any other would have suffered, 2 Sam. 12:1-15. David's true devotion to God is revealed in the Psalms.
3. Polygamy, as practiced by Jacob, Elkanah, David, Solomon, etc. Again, let it be remembered that the Bible does not encourage polygamy. The Bible reveals that in every polygamous home there was unhappiness, which is boldly pictured.
4. Concubines and the laws of Moses concerning concubinage. Here again the Bible seeks to regulate an existing social custom without endorsing it. Slavery, which is mentioned in both the Old and New Testaments, but is never outrightly condemned. Nor is it sanctioned, but regulated with a high ethical standard.

CONCLUSION:

The Christian's question is, How could a perfect moral standard have been the outgrowth of falsehood, deception and fraud, perpetrated over a period of fifteen hundred years, with never a discordant note, a contradiction in doctrine, or false note in its ethical code?

His conclusion is: The Bible is a Special Divine Revelation!

Lesson 10
Its Relevancy to Human Needs

Man is a dual being, physical and moral or spiritual. In the material world there is that which satisfies and gratifies every physical desire of man. There is not a physical appetite that cannot be gratified by the world of physical things. But – there is that about man which all the physical and material things of earth cannot satisfy. There is a constant longing, a hungering for something beyond the merely physical. These are recognized as religious or spiritual needs.

Does Christianity provide for all of man's spiritual needs? This becomes the question of this lesson. It claims to make such provision, Matt. 5:6; John 1:16-18; Col. 2:9, 10. If it does fulfill such desires and longings, this becomes evidence that both the physical world and the Bible are from a common source; that the author of both had a perfect knowledge of the needs of man physically and spiritually. If the Bible does not meet these spiritual needs, it fails of its own claim. Is it then worth defending?

IT SOLVES PROBLEMS OTHERWISE UNSOLVABLE

1. The problem of man's origin, purpose and destiny. Human philosophies offer guesses and theories respecting the origin and destiny of beings and things; e.g., the theory of evolution. The Bible alone gives a rational answer to the problem, as it declares the universe to be the product of an intelligent Creator, Gen. 1-2; destined to an end determined by character: righteousness or sin, Rev. 20-22.
2. The problem of myths and traditions: a fall, flood, tower and confusion, origin of nations. These myths would be unintelligible were it not for the Bible's declaration of an actual fact out of which these

Internal Evidences of Christianity   48

grew.

IT PROVIDES A BEING WORTHY OF WORSHIP: GOD

1. Man will have an object of worship; he is "incurably religious."
2. God as He is revealed in the Bible is *personal* and *moral*. Therefore a Being with whom man can have fellowship and communion.
3. He became incarnate in His Son, giving to man a perfect revelation of His character and nature. Perfect in wisdom, power and holiness, He becomes a being worthy of man's worship and adoration.

IT MEETS THE DESIRE TO BE RIGHT WITH ONE'S MAKER

1. Since man must have an object of worship, when he forsook God in early ages, he created gods in his own image. The sacrifices of the ages have been attempts on man's part to find peace with his God or God.
2. The *fact* of sin, whether or not one accepts the Bible account of it, cannot be denied. Sin and its consequences in human experience are a present and patent fact. Sin separates man from his God or God.
3. Though the Bible presents God in absolute holiness and righteousness, and sin as separating man from God (Isa. 59:1-2); its theme is one of reconciliation, a reconciliation which provides peace with Him, Rom. 5:1-2; 2 Cor. 5:18-19; Eph. 2:1123; I John 2:1-2.
4. Through this reconciliation, fellowship and communion with God are enjoyed by the individual, I John 1:3, 4; I Cor. 1:9.

IT COMPLEMENTS MAN'S CONSCIOUS WEAKNESS

1. In a world of sin, death and decay, man feels alone and weak. Regeneration, a distinctive characteristic of the Christian religion, corrects this, implanting a new principle of life, John 3:3; Titus 3:5; 2 Cor. 5:16, 17.
2. Through the indwelling Christ, Eph. 3:14-19, the "new creature" has strength for every need, Eph. 3:20-21; Phil. 4:13; I Cor. 10:13; 2 Cor. 12:9.
3. Other systems, Mohammedanism, Buddhism, etc., fail to effect any permanent transformation of the hearts and lives of men. The gospel method, when honestly and seriously applied, never fails. It provides love, and a standard of right relations to one's fellow-man.

IT AFFORDS COMFORT IN TRIAL

1. Whether in sickness, misfortune, or bereavement, the Bible comforts the heart of the sufferer, John 14:1-3; Rom. 8:28; 15:4; 2 Cor. 4:17; Heb. 12:11, etc.

IT CANCELS THE FEAR OF DEATH

1. Although the Christian may "dread" death, the "fear" is destroyed by the gospel, 2 Tim. 1:10; John 14:1-3; 2 Cor. 5:1ff; I Cor. 15; etc.

IT FITS INTO MAN'S COMPLEX PSYCHOLOGY

1. The Bible appeals to and is fitted for man's intellect, affections and will. It meets his spiritual and ethical needs of mind, desire and realization.
2. It is corrective, making the proud humble, the hating to love, the covetous to sacrifice, this proves the author to have had a perfect understanding of man and of all his needs.

References:
H.W. Everest, *The Divine Demonstration,* pp. 172-198.
Fundamentals, Vol. III., p. 86-87
Floyd Hamilton, *The Basis of Christian Faith*, pp. 132-149.
L.S. Keyser, *System of Christian Evidence*, pp. 87-95.
E.Y. Mullins, *Why Is Christianity True?,* pp. 396-412

Lesson 11
The Historical Trustworthiness of the Bible

"The Bible claims to be a historical book. It claims to be a record of what has actually happened in the past. It is... the *History of Redemption*... A book may be historically accurate and not be inspired, but no book can be accepted as inspired which is found to be historically inaccurate. If the Bible is the Word of God, it must be historically accurate." – Hamilton, *Basis of Christian Faith,* pp. 165, 6. See also Bernard Ramm, *Protestant Christian Evidences,* p. 25.

If the Bible cannot be trusted in this point, i.e., of historical trustworthiness, it cannot be trusted in any. *It must* be historically accurate. This does not prove it inspired, but adds to the testimony which would lend to such a conclusion.

THE HISTORICAL ACCURACY OF THE OLD TESTAMENT

1. It is impossible to test the Bible in every point because of lack of external materials. "We claim that if we can show that the Bible documents are historically accurate in those places where we can test them by external evidence, we have a right to assume their accuracy in those places where external evidence is lacking one way or the other, until further evidence proving their inaccuracy is discovered" (Hamilton, *op. cit.,* p. 171).
2. Topographical and geographical trustworthiness of the Bible. As excavations are made, every discovery is in harmony with fact as it is presented in the Bible.
3. The ethnological correctness of Scripture. Here

Internal Evidences of Christianity 52

again every discovery made corroborates the table of nations, Gen. 10, and other places. See Free, *Archaeology and Bible History,* pp. 44, 45, and the book by a symposium of writers.

EXAMPLES OF THE BIBLICAL CORRECTNESS AS PROVED BY DISCOVERIES

1. Narrative in Gen. 14, concerning the alliance between Elam and Shinar: "All the evidence on the subject that has come to light has supported the narrative and not one bit of evidence tending to discredit the story has been discovered" (Hamilton, *op. cit.,* p. 177. See also Free, pp. 57-58).
2. The Exodus narrative. Pithom was discovered by Prof. Naville in 1883; and the ruins were examined by Prof. Kyle in 1908. Kyle describes the brick in the buildings as found in Exodus: brick with straw, brick with stubble, and brick with neither. It was the city built by the Israelites. (See Free, pp. 85-86).
3. Belshazzar, son of Nabonidus, grandson of Nebuchadnezzar by a daughter. Tablets show Nabonidus was king, but away on a campaign and Belshazzar was co-regent with his father. Only place he could have offered Daniel was that of third in the government. (See Free, pp. 232-255).
4. Historical names of kings. 41 of the number mentioned from Abraham to the end of the Old Testament have been found in contemporary documents. Perfect agreement! (See Hamilton).

HISTORICAL ACCURACY OF THE NEW TESTAMENT

1. Explorations of the country discover the cities and villages as mentioned and located in the New Testament. All that have been identified are as located in the N. T.
2. Book of Acts. Discoveries made by Sir William

Ramsay confirm all of Luke's statements of places, rulers, titles, etc. Not a conflict!

References:
- Wm. F. Albright, *From the Stone Age to Christianity,* (Anchor Edition), p. 1-23, 24, 81.
- George A. Barton, *Archaeology and the Bible,* p. 13-30, 61-73, 455-480.
- Joseph P. Free, *Archaeology and Bible History,* pp. 44, 45, 57f, 130-132, 232-235.
- Floyd Hamilton, *Basis of Christian Faith,* p. 164-193 (read all of this chapter).
- Symposium of writers, *Modern Science and Christian Faith,* "Anthropology" 98-193.

Lesson 12
Scientific Accuracy of the Bible

Probably the greatest objection offered today against the Bible is that it is not "scientific," that it contradicts scientific truth. This we deny. The Bible, though not weighted down with scientific terms of the present century, is scientifically accurate in its statements and teaching. A conflict between scientific facts and the teaching of the Scriptures has never been established. Three points to be noted: 1. The Bible and theories of science may conflict. 2. Facts of science and theories of the Bible may conflict. 3. Truth of the Bible and facts of science do not conflict.

Physical science has to do with phenomenon, facts and laws of nature; the Bible with morals, ideals and the conscience. "True science seeks to 'think God's thoughts after Him"... It is knowledge validated and classified" (Keyser, *op. cit.,* p. 182). The conflict is between the Bible and human speculations, not between the Bible and validated facts, or, between erroneous interpretations of the Bible and science. "Science shows the method of the world, but not its cause; the Bible shows its cause but not its method." Therefore let the Bible and science remain in the field of each. Shepfer, *The Bible and Science,* p. 176.

WE AFFIRM THAT PERFECT HARMONY EXISTS BETWEEN SCRIPTURE AND SCIENCE

Harry Rimmer summarizes the evidence for this affirmation under four propositions:
1. Proposition 1. "The Bible *does* contain scientific truth even though its facts are stated in non-scientific language." (Some of these truths we shall consider under heading II.)
2. Proposition 2. "The Bible *does not* contain the errors and fallacies of science common to the age of its production." The writers of Scripture lived in

successive stages of culture, and wrote under its influence:
   a. Moses. "And Moses was instructed (learned) in all the wisdom of the Egyptians" (Acts 7:22), yet there is not to be found in any of his writings the theories of the Egyptians concerning the beginning of the world from a flying egg, or the origin of man from the white worms of the Nile. Instead, Gen. 1:1; 2:7; etc.
   b. Daniel. The Babylonians sought him because of his wisdom, not he for theirs. The crudities of Babylonian myths do not enter into his writings.
   c. Prophets of all the periods. They stood out against the false wisdom of their day, writing only that which has since harmonized with scientific truth, never allowing the errors of the day to become part of the record.
3. Proposition 3. "The Bible is in harmony with modern science in the remarkable fashion in which it disagrees with modern error, exactly as it has contradicted ancient fallacy." Evolution, as an example. This is purely theory, not a science. Facts do not support it. Three points in which evolution fails to take into account new factors in creation:
   a. The transition from inorganic to organic existence, the entrance of *life.*
   b. The transition from purely organic development to *consciousness.*
   c. The transition to rationality, personality, and moral life in man.
4. Proposition 4. "The Bible is in harmony with modern science, in that it has anticipated many of the discoveries of these recent centuries." This raises the issue: Did the Biblical writers know these things of which they wrote as a matter of wisdom and knowledge of the day, or were they inspired?

(This affirmation by Mr. Rimmer may be challenged; in places it is very weak. H. H.) (Rimmer, *The Harmony of Science and Scripture,* pp. 60-78. Read this chapter.)

WE CONCLUDE THAT SUCH SCIENTIFIC ACCURACY MARKS THE BIBLE AS A BOOK DISTINCT FROM ALL OTHER WRITINGS OF ITS DAY.

(Rimmer, *ibid.*)

1. *Waters in one place [bed] -seas,* Gen. 1:9, 10. Seas, plural, but all are connected, hence "one bed."
2. *Northern void, gravity, Job 26:7.* These two ideas are presented at a time when ordinarily men thought the earth to be flat and resting upon something.
3. *Sea not full,* Ecc. 1:7. 186,000 cubic miles of water flow annually into the seas, and for millenniums. Today scientists can explain the mystery of evaporation and the cycle of water. This writer shows a knowledge of such which amazes us.
4. *Germs* and the gauze mask, Lev. 13:45. What was known of such as germs?
5. *One blood,* Acts 17:26 (cf. A.V. and Am. Std. V.); Lev. 17:11; Deut. 12:23. Here the essential nature of the blood is clearly revealed; yet little was known about it till recent years.
6. *Various kinds of flesh,* I Cor. 15:39. Modern science confirms Paul's claims.

References:
H.W. Everest, *op. cit.,* pp. 107-199.
Fundamentals, Vol. IV, pp. 91-104.
L.S. Keyser, *Op. Cit.,* pp. 182-185.
Modern Science and the Christian Faith, Chapters IV, VII, VIII.
Harry Rimmer, *Modern Science and the Genesis Record.*

Harry Rimmer, *Harmony of Science and Scripture,* Chapters 1-4. Wilbur M. Smith, *Therefore Stand,* pp. 272-358.

PART THREE – FULFILLED PROPHECY

Lesson 13
Israel's History

One of the strongest arguments for the proposition of the course, The Bible a Special Divine Revelation, is the fulfilled prophecies of the Old and New Covenants. The proposition may be stated thus:

1. Man cannot know the future; only God can foretell history or events.
2. The Bible foretold the destiny of nations and the coming of Christ.
3. Therefore, the Bible is the word of God, not of man.

Only the second, or minor premise must be proved. The first is accepted.

Everest says, "The criteria of true prophecy are the following: (1) The event must be beyond the power of man to foresee... (2) It must be demonstrated that the prediction was written before the event. (3) The prediction must be applicable to the event. (4) The prediction must be unambiguous and unmistakable. ("It must contain a sufficient number of details to exclude accident or guesswork," Rimmer). (5) The prediction must have a clear and demonstrable fulfilment" (H.W. Everest, *The Divine Demonstration,* p. 260).

God has declared His power to foretell events; and upon this power and ability God rested His claim to be the one God, Isa. 41:1-8, 21-26; 42:8; 44:6-8; 46:8-11; 48:3. Study carefully and thoroughly these passages from Isaiah. Further, God has told man how he is to discern true prophecy from false, Jer. 28:7-9; Deut. 18:20-22.

BALAAM'S PROPHECY CONCERNING ISRAEL
PROOF OF INSPIRATION
(Numbers 23, 24). (From Everest)
1. Israel was to dwell alone, separate from other nations, 23:9.

Israel's History

2. Israel was to become a numerous people, 23:10; see also Gen. 12:1-3.
3. Israel should become powerful, "a lion," 23:24; 24:8, 9.
4. An eminent and powerful king should appear, 24:17.
5. This ruler should conquer Moab, Edom, and Amalek, 24:17b-20. David did appear and conquer, 2 Sam. 8:13-17; I Kings 11:15-16. Revolt under Joram, 2 Kings 8:20-22. Subdued under Christ, Amos 9:11-12; Obadiah 17ff.
6. The Kenites should be preserved and become servants of the Jews, 24:21-22.
7. Asshur (Assyria) should carry Israel into captivity, 24:22. (10 tribes, Assyrian captivity, 722 B.C.)

THE HISTORY OF ISRAEL, WRITTEN FIFTEEN HUNDRED YEARS IN THE FUTURE, PROVES THE BOOK A SPECIAL DIVINE REVELATION

(Lev. 26; Deut. 28) The Mosaic authorship of Deuteronomy is taken for granted, since it has never been disproved. The internal, external and incidental testimony all confirm the claim that Moses wrote it. Should the student be interested in a study of the authorship, he may consult McGarvey, *The Authorship of Deuteronomy;* James Orr, *The Problem of the Old Testament;* W.H. Green, *Moses and the Prophets;* Young, *Introduction to the Old Testament;* article in (*I S.B.E.*)

1. Blessings upon Israel if they should be obedient to Jehovah, Deut. 28:1-14.
2. Cursings if disobedient, which becomes their "history foretold," 28:14-64.
   a. Foretold about 400 years in advance that they should have a king, v. 36.
   b. They should become a "hiss and a byword," v. 37; Jer. 29:18.

Internal Evidences of Christianity 62

    c. A nation from afar to come against them: vv. 49, 50. Assyria, Babylonia and Rome fit the description and all came against her.
    d. Great sufferings to accompany the siege, in which siege they should eat their young, vv. 53, 56-57. Syria, 2 Kings 6:24-31; Babylon, Lamentations 2:20; 4:10; Rome, Josephus. (See Josephus, *Wars,* Bk. 6, ch. 3, par. 4, p. 818).
    e. Their end should be one most fearful, vv. 64-67.
    f. They should be scattered, taken captive, sold till none would want to buy them -a glutted market, v. 68. (Josephus, *Ibid.,* B. 6, ch. 9, par. 2, p. 831).
3. Although they would be scattered, they should never be consumed, Jer. 5:18; 30:11. They should never again be a kingdom, Jer. 19:10-11. Always a people; but never a kingdom.
4. The Restored Remnant
    a. When they should become disobedient they would be scattered, Deut. 30:1-11.
    b. A remnant would return, Isa. 10:20-23; Jer. 23:1-3; after seventy years, Jer. 25:12; 29:10.
    c. The remnant did return, Ezra 1:1-4; 2:70; 9:6-9, 13-15; Neh. 1:2-10; 9:7-8; Haggai 1:12; 1:14; 2:2; Zech. 8:6, 11-12. 5. The Jews therefore are even now a monument to God's divine providence, and to the divine inspiration of the Scriptures.

References:
    A. Alexander, *Evidences,* p. 130-169.
    H.W. Everest, *The Divine Demonstration,* p. 257-359.
    G.P. Fisher, *Manual of Christian Evidences*, p. 95-98.
    Foster, *Studies in Theology,* Vol. III, p. 70-165.
    Floyd Hamilton, *The Basis of Christian Faith*, p. 296-317.

C.E. MacCartney, *Christian Faith and the Spirit of the Age*, p. 81-105.
B. Ramm, *Protestant Christian Evidences*, 51-124.
Harry Rimmer, *Internal Evidence of Inspiration*, p. 183-223.
Urquhort, *Wonders of Prophecy*.
Edward Young, *Isaiah 53*.

Lesson 14
The Nations

Although in a special way the Scriptures have to do with the history of the Jews, they by no means ignore the nations among whom Israel was cast. The fulfilled prophecies concerning Israel, and the presence of the Jews among us today, present a powerful argument in behalf of our proposition, The Scriptures a Special Divine Revelation. No less impressive and strong is the testimony of the fulfilled prophecies regarding the nations among whom Israel as a people dwelt.

As God foretold the continued existence of Israel as a people, He also foretold the "full end" of the nations, Jer. 30:11; 46:28. The Jews are here today; the nations are not here. Both facts are monuments to the inspiration of the prophecies. A few of the prophecies concerning some of these nations are here briefly considered.

PROPHECIES CONCERNING EGYPT
(Isaiah 19; Ezekiel 29:30)
1. Egypt was to become desolate in the midst of desolations.
2. There should be no more a prince of Egypt; it was to be ruled by strangers. "Egypt has had many different masters through the centuries since the time of the prophecy. First the Babylonians, then the Persians, then the Greeks, the Romans, the Arabs, the Turks, the French, and lastly the English, but all have been strangers and all have despoiled the land of its riches" (Hamilton, *Basis of Christian Faith,* p. 304).
3. It was to become the basest of kingdoms. The land was to become less productive, Ezek. 30:12; Isa. 19:5, 6. Modern writers say the Nile now supports only a fraction of the former land it supplied and

Internal Evidences of Christianity

irrigated. The canals have been diminished and dried up.
4. Idolatry was to be destroyed. Yet, Egypt should be redeemed.

PROPHECY CONCERNING NINEVEH
(Isa. 10:12-14; Zeph. 2:13-15; book of Nahum)
1. This great and flourishing city was to be destroyed.
2. It was to be captured when its rulers and defenders were drunken.
3. Destruction should not rise up a second time.
4. It should become a desolation and dry, like a wilderness or desert.
5. Flocks should lie down there. Those who passed by should hiss and wag the head in sympathy with the ruin which had mocked its former grandeur.

PROPHECY CONCERNING BABYLON
(Isa. 13:1-14:27; Jer. 50, 51)

It was to be entirely overthrown, as were Sodom and Gomorrah. The Medes were to be the destroyers of Babylon (Isa. 13:17-19; Jer. 51:11, 28).
1. It should never be inhabited nor dwelt in from generation to generation.
2. The Arab should not pitch tent there; nor shepherds make their folds.
3. Wild beasts of the desert should lie there.
4. Her walls and foundations and palaces should be cast into heaps.
5. The sower and the harvester should be cut off.
6. These who passed by should be astonished at her plagues.

PROPHECY CONCERNING TYRE
(Isa. 23; Ezek. 26:1-28:19; Zech. 9:3, 4)
1. The city was to be taken and destroyed by the Chaldeans, Ezek. 26:7-11.

2. Again Tyre was to be taken and destroyed. Ezek. 27:32; Zech. 9:3, 4. Alexander the Great was the second destroyer, 332 B. C.
3. Finally, the city should become a place where fishermen would dry their nets.

PROPHECY CONCERNING SIDON
(Ezek. 28:20-24)
1. It should be a scene of bloodshed and slaughter.
2. Not said of Sidon as of Tyre, that it should be utterly destroyed or not rebuilt. "Blood has flowed in the streets again and again, but the city stands today, a monument to fulfilled prophecy. Now suppose Tyre and Sidon had exchanged places in the prophecy... Suppose it had been said of Sidon, "Thou shall be built no more!" What would have become of the prophecy? How does it happen there was not such an exchange?" (Hamilton, *op. cit.,* p. 300).

Lesson 15
Christ in Prophecy

The fact that the Old Testament was complete several hundred years before Christ was born, yet so perfectly points to Him that in all points He fulfills the predictions, is proof conclusive that God inspired the ancient writers. In this outline Everest is followed.

JESUS AND THE APOSTLES CLAIMED THAT CHRIST FULFILLED PROPHECIES
1. The Old Testament promised the coming of a Messiah, Gen. 3:15; 12:3; 2 Samuel 7:1213; Jeremiah 23:5, 6; Isaiah 9:6; Mal. 3:1.
2. Jesus claimed to fulfill prophecy, John 5:39; 5:46; Lk. 24:44, 45.
3. The apostles made the same claim for Him, Acts 3:18, 21, 24; 10:43; 13:27; 17:2.

THE *TIME* OF THE MESSIAH'S COMING CLEARLY FORETOLD:
1. "Last days," Isa. 2:2; Joel 2:28; Dan. 2:28.
2. During the days of the fourth empire (Roman), Dan. 2:31-45; Luke 2:1.
3. Before Judah should cease as a distinct people, Gen. 49:10.
4. "In the fulness of time" (fulness of things spoken by the prophets), Gal. 4:4.

THE *PLACE* OF THE MESSIAH'S NATIVITY DECLARED
1. Micah 5:2; Matt. 2:1.

THE *LINEAGE* OF THE MESSIAH WAS DECLARED IN SCRIPTURE:
1. To be a descendent of Abraham, Gen. 12:3; 22:18;

Cf. Gal. 3:8-16; 4:4.
2. Of the tribe of Judah, Gen. 49:10.
3. Of the house of David, 2 Samuel 7:12, 13; 23:1-7; Isa. 11:1, 2, 11; Acts 13:22-23.
4. His human nature to be derived from woman, Gen. 3:15; Gal. 4:4; Matt. 1:18-21.

HE SHOULD PARTAKE OF *THE DIVINE NATURE:*
1. "My son," Ps. 2:7; see Matt. 3:17; 17:5. "From everlasting," Micah 5:2.
2. To be equal with God: "my fellow," Zech. 13:7. Fellow, "i.e.,, one united by community of nature... God speaks of the Shepherd who was slain as 'my fellow, united in nature with Himself'" (Pusey, *Minor Prophets,* Vol. II, p. 445. See also Phil. 2:6; John 10:30).

THE *CHARACTER* OF THE MESSIAH MINUTELY DESCRIBED BY THE PROPHETS:
1. His obedience, Deut. 18:18; see John 6:38; 12:49; 15:15; Lk. 22:42; Heb. 5:7-9.
2. His wisdom, Isa. 11:1-4.
3. His love for righteousness, Ps. 45:7.
4. His gentleness and tenderness, Isa. 42:1-4. His compassion, Isa. 61:1-3. See Luke 4:21.
5. His piety, Ps. 40:7, 8. See Heb. 10:7.

SOME *MAIN EVENTS* IN THE LIFE OF JESUS MINUTELY AND ACCURATELY PREDICTED:
1. A divinely appointed harbinger was to announce His coming, Mal. 3:1; 4:5; Isa. 40:3. See Luke 1:17; Matt. 17:9-13; Mark 9:9-13.
2. To be annointed with the Holy Spirit, Isa. 42:1; 61:1. See Matt. 3:16, 17.
3. To enter upon His ministry in Galilee, Isa. 9:1-2; see Matt. 4:12-16.
4. He should be a "man of sorrows," Isa. 53:3.

5. To enter Jerusalem in triumph, Zech. 9:9; but should be rejected by the Jewish people, Isa. 53:1-3; see John 1:11; Matt. 21:4-5; 27:22, 23.

THE *BETRAYAL* AND *TRIAL* OF THE MESSIAH
1. The betrayal, Zech. 11:12, 13.
2. His demeanor when on trial, Isa. 53:7.

THE CRUCIFIXION AND BURIAL
1. To die by an unjust judgment, Isa. 53:8; crucifixion, Ps. 22:15-18. 'See John 19:23, 24.
2. To be scourged preparatory to the crucifixion, Isa. 50:6. Read also Psalm 22; all of Isaiah 53.

THE RESURRECTION, ASCENSION, AND CORONATION OF THE MESSIAH
1. Messiah to rise from the dead, Isa. 53:10, 11; Ps. 16:10; 2:6,7.
2. To ascend on high, Ps. 68:18; 24:7.
3. To be crowned with power and glory, Dan. 7:13, 14.

THE *OFFICES* OF THE MESSIANIC KINGDOM FILLED BY JESUS:
1. The kingdom should be one of peace, Isa. 9:6, 7; 11:5-6; 2:2-4.
2. Jesus to be King, Ps. 2:6; 110:2, 3.
3. Priest, Ps. 110:4; Zech. 6:12, 13.
4. Prophet, Deut. 18:15-19; Acts 3:22-23; Hebrews 1:1-3.

CONCLUSION:
Only a divine mind could have conceived such a character through the centuries, recording these things about Him; and only a divine person could have fulfilled the predictions. Therefore: *Jesus is the Christ of God and The Bible is a Special Divine Revelation!*

PART FOUR – JESUS CHRIST

Lesson 16
Jesus Christ – "Who Say Ye That I Am?"

Jesus Christ cannot be ignored! His friends love Him and His enemies hate Him, but all must acknowledge the fact of His existence. Keyser says, "The crucial question is, *Could mere human wisdom have conceived and depicted such a character*" (A System of Christian Evidence, p. 96).

He demands an explanation. Also, He demands an attitude on our part. Every individual develops an attitude toward Him, upon which depends the eternal destiny of the soul. Modern Bible critics are prone to ascribe to Him a place lower than that of deity; they say, "He is earth's greatest man, its greatest teacher, greatest philosopher; He has revealed God to us as no one else has." But beyond this they do not go. To them He is "a good, a great man," but no more.

The question of supreme moment becomes, "Who say ye that I am?" He is the Christ or He *is not* a good man, is the proposition of this lesson.

A CONSIDERATION OF THE *CHARGES* MADE AGAINST HIM HELPS TO ANSWER THE QUESTION

1. He loved sinners and ate with them. This He admitted.
2. He healed on the Sabbath. Yes, for it is always right to do good.
3. He claimed to be King. Yes, but not in competition with Caesar, John 18.
4. Blasphemy – Son of God -John 10:30-35 – But was the evidence sufficient to prove Him a blasphemer?

A CONSIDERATION OF HIS *CLAIMS* HELPS TO ANSWER THE QUESTION

1. He claimed equality with God, John 5:17-18

Who is Jesus?

   a. In the next breath He claimed power greater than that previously exercised by God, John 5:19-20. He would give spiritual life, raise the dead, and act as judge, vv. 2229.
   b. No wonder the Jews sought to stone Him! His claim to equality with God, John 10:27-33.
   c. He declared that to see Him is to see the Father, John 14:7-10.
   d. He confessed Himself to be the Christ, "The Son of the Blessed," Mark 14:61-64.
   e. Conclusion: In the light of these claims, He is the CHRIST or an impudent PRETENDER. There is no middle ground. He is not merely a "good man."
2. He accepted worship:
   a. Jesus taught that only God is to receive worship.
   b. But – during His ministry He accepted worship from a leper, Matt. 8:2; a ruler of the synagogue, Matt. 9:18: the blind man made to see, John 9:35-38.
   c. After His resurrection, He received worship from the disciples, Matt. 28:9; and from Thomas, accepting His confession of Lordship and Godhood, John 20:26-29.
3. Conclusion: In accepting worship, knowing only God is to be worshiped, He is either a DIVINE BEING or a BLASPHEMER.

A CONSIDERATION OF HIS *CHARACTER* HELPS TO ANSWER THE QUESTION

1. Compare Him with the millions since Adam; He is the *one* UNIVERSAL character.
2. Compare Him with His Apostles:
   a. *Paul* confessed himself the "chief of sinners," I Tim. 1:15.
   b. *Peter* asked the Lord to depart from him, a

Internal Evidences of Christianity 76

sinful man, Luke 5:8.
- c. *John* says anyone who says he has not sinned makes God a liar, I John 1:8-10.
- d. But Jesus confessed no sin, and challenged His adversaries to convict Him of sin, John 8:46. How is this difference to be explained? Was His standard of right lower than theirs? or was His standard of life higher? should be worshiped, Matt. 4:10; John 4:23.

3. *He claimed sinlessness* in His challenge to His enemies, John 8:46; yet,
    - a. He condemned self-righteousness, Luke 18:9-14, but confessed no sin himself.
    - b. Conclusion: He is the CHRIST or a HYPOCRITE. There is no middle ground.
4. He claimed to be "light," "way," "the good shepherd," etc.
5. John 8:12; 10:10, 11, 16; 14:6. If all this, He is the Saviour of man; He is the CHRIST. If not, He is a LIAR and an IMPOSTER. Again, no middle ground.
6. He allowed the Apostles to believe Him to be the Christ, declaring that upon the truth of this proposition He would build the church, Matt. 16:16-18. In allowing them to believe such, either He was the CHRIST or He was a DECEIVER. Nineteen centuries have confirmed the truth of His claim.
7. *He claimed His blood should seal His teaching and procure remission of sins* Matt. 26:28; 20:28. He died for this belief and cause; was it true or was it falsehood? Surely He believed it. Believing such, He was the CHRIST, the SON OF GOD, or a FANATIC. Who do you say that He was and is?

References:
Fundamentals, Vol. VI, pp. 64-84.

Mark Hopkins, *Evidences of Christianity,* pp. 217-237.
L.S. Keyser, *op. Cit.,* pp. 96-97.
J. Gresham Machen, *Christianity and Liberalism*, pp. 80-116.
Harry Rimmer, *Internal Evidence of Inspiration*, pp. 149-179.

Lesson 17
Jesus Christ — The Universal Character

In this lesson, and several to follow, the purpose is to show that the uniqueness of Jesus Christ proves Him to be the Son of God. Nothing is assumed; the Four Gospels are here. We propose to look at the picture therein presented and raise the question, Did Jesus actually live or was He invented? If He lived, how shall we account for the uniqueness of His character and His influence upon history except on the ground that He was divine, the Son of God. Based on the evidence found, we affirm that it is more rational to believe that He was what He claimed to be, than to believe any other explanation offered. (The following outline is based on *The Man of Galilee,* by A.G. Haygood.)

DID THE EVANGELISTS INVENT JESUS?
1. The four Gospels are here; they present a character who lives in the literature and history of the centuries, and in the lives of men today. Did these four men invent Jesus? If "yes," then they have performed a miracle greater than any ascribed to Jesus, for they have created the one perfect character, teaching a perfect system of morals, and one who lived every point that He taught. A mighty miracle indeed!
2. Matthew, Mark, Luke, John neither good nor great enough for the task.
    a. Measure the evangelists' *thoughts* by Jesus and His thoughts:
        i. Of the kingdom. Jesus: kingdom of heaven; Disciples: kingdom of Israel, with themselves in places of greatness, Mark 10:35-45; Matt. 20:20-28.
        ii. Of suffering, sacrifice, self-denial, Matt. 16:21-26; 26:36, 51-52; John 18:10, 11.

Internal Evidences of Christianity 80

      iii. Of false teaching. Jesus: of hypocrisy; disciples of "bread," Matt. 16:512.
   b. Measure their *courage* with that of Jesus; theirs was physical, his was moral. They could fight with the sword, but shrank from criticism; Jesus veered not a hair's breadth from truth, under any circumstance, Matt. 26:31-35, 51-56, 69-75.
   c. Measure and compare the two conceptions *of brotherhood,* Luke 9:51-56; 19:1-10; John 4; 8:1-11.
3. The characters of historians, biographers, fiction writers bear the impress of the writers or of individuals of the period. Compare Shakespeare's characters, Milton's Satan, the characters of his biographers or of the period. Jesus stands alone. We conclude: The Evangelists did NOT invent Jesus.

IS JESUS AN IDEAL JEW OF ANY AGE OF HEBREW HISTORY?
1. Jesus was not a Jew peculiar to the Age of Tiberius.
   a. He was not the Nation's ideal of a hero and deliverer; He utterly spoiled their idea of a Messiah, John 6:15; 18:33-38. He refused their crown, so they crucified Him.
   b. The Jews hated Samaritans; Jesus used them to illustrate His lessons of brotherhood, Luke 10:25-37, and of thanksgiving, Luke 17:11-19; etc.
   c. The Jews of Jesus' day were dominated by the master passion of patriotism; they hated Rome. Jesus taught them to "love your enemies," Matt. 5:43-48; and to pay tribute to Caesar, Matt. 22:15-22.
2. Jesus was not a product of mythology. He violates every rule and law of myths:
   a. Myths originate and, as conceptions, are

complete before written history.
  b. About all myths there is something grotesque, if not monstrous. They are exaggerations of men or animals; gigantic, strange, unnatural, impossible. But Jesus appears as a man, simply; nothing exaggerated or unnatural. Not so much as a word about His personal appearance.
  c. Myths reflect their *time, place,* and *race.* This statement is without exception. Compare the various gods of the different ancients, how like the people are they! But in Jesus there is no trace of Hebrew coloring from any period.
  d. In all nations, myths defy *chronology:* they are without dates; they appear before any history. The people date them from their very beginning. Find one that appears at a definite date. But not so of Jesus, definite dates are fixed, Luke 2:1-2; Matt. 2:1, etc.
  e. Myths defy *topography* as they do chronology: not only are they without location, but without dates. Not so of Jesus, John 7:27, etc.
  f. Myths are not completed at once; they require long ages for development. But Jesus comes into history suddenly, and has remained unchanged since first He appeared; He is today as he appeared in the gospels.
  g. All myths belong to the *infancy,* never to the old age of a nation. Consistent with this principle, He should have come before Abraham. Instead, He appears at the close of Hebrew history.
3. Jesus was not a product of Hebrew human nature. Compare Him with:
  a. Hebrew fathers: Abraham, Isaac, Jacob, David – does He fit in as one of them? We judge a tree by its fruit; could the tree that produced them have produced Him?

b. Hebrew statesmen, lawgivers, priests, soldiers, kings, all.
  c. Compare Him with men of all nations of all ages; is He one of them? – He stands alone.

References:
L. Boettner. *Studies in Theology,* p. 140-269.
G.P. Fisher. *Manual of Christian Evidences.*
The Fundamentals. Vols. III. IV.
A.G. Haygood, *The Man of Galilee.*
John Marquis, *Learning to Teach from the Master Teacher.*
E.Y. Muffins, *Why is Christianity True?*
C.A. Row, *A Manual of Christian Evidences*

Lesson 18
Jesus Christ — His Moral Glory

The summary of this topic and the proposition of this study have been well stated by another who wrote, "His moral glory consists of the perfections which marked His earthly life and ministry; perfections which attached to every relation He sustained, and to every circumstance in which He was found." The proposition is, "The moral glory of Jesus Christ as set forth in the four Gospels cannot be the product of the unaided human intellect, that only the Spirit of God is competent to execute this matchless portrait of the Son of Man" (W.G. Morehead, *The Fundamentals,* Vol. III, p. 42).

Some of the relations of Christ which reveal His perfections are here set forth:

I. HIS RELATION TO SIN
1. What is Sin? Transgression of law – I John 3:4; failure to do good, James 4:17. Jesus never confessed sin, although He denounced self-righteousness and commended confession, Luke 18:9-14. Jesus was tempted in all points as others, but while condemning all sin, John 8:24, 44, He challenged anyone to point to a sin in His life, John 8:46.
2. Jesus forgave sin. He was merciful to sinners, John 8:11; forgave sins and worked a miracle to establish His claim, Mark 2:1-12.
3. He gave Himself for the sins of others, shedding His blood to the end that sins might be remitted, Matt. 16:21-24; 20:28; 26:28. John 3:14-19; 6:51; 10:15, 17; 12:32-33. Who is this to sustain such a relation to sin?

HIS RELATION TO LAW
1. Such a relation to sin suggests at once a relation to the law of which sin is a violation. Jesus contrasted himself with all other moral teachers, "I say unto you," "These sayings of mine," etc., Matt. 5-7.
2. Jesus fulfilled the law, Matt. 5:17, 18; cf. the book of Hebrews.
3. He openly declared Himself Lord, Matt. 7:22; greater than the temple, Matt. 12:6; Lord of the Sabbath, Matt. 12:8; greater than Jonah, Matt. 12:38-41; and that He is to be Judge of all, John 12:48-49; Matt. 25:31-47.

HIS RELATION TO THE KINGDOM OF GOD
1. The idea of law belongs to a kingdom in which it operates: physical, civil, spiritual. What is His relation to the Spiritual, the kingdom of God?
2. The idea of kingdom is central in the teaching of Jesus. He taught that the kingdom was "at hand," Matt. 4:17; 6:10; Mark 1:14, 15, "cometh without observation," "is among or in the midst of you," Luke 17:20-21, and that it is spiritual, John 18:36.
3. Jesus claimed Himself "Lord," Matt. 7:22; confessed Himself "King," Luke 23:3; declared the nature of the King and Kingdom, John 8:36-38; announced the conditions of membership in the kingdom, and the rewards of those laboring therein, and the principles on which they are to be bestowed. "What manner of man is this who assumes the position of sovereignty in the religious realm and who discharges an office which seems no less than divine in a world of spiritual forces?" (E.Y. Mullins, *Why Is Christianity True? p.* 103)

HIS RELATION TO PROVIDENCE
1. Out of His declarations concerning the kingdom arises the question of Providence. Can He control

Jesus' Moral Glory

events and forces in the world and carry His kingdom to its consummation? His own answer is clear and confident, Matt. 24, 25.
2. Jesus predicted in outline the spiritual history of the race and claimed that His own was the hand upon the helm guiding to the destined haven, Matt. 28:18-20.

HIS RELATION TO THE FORCES OF NATURE
1. Back of Providence is another world of forces to be dealt with; the cosmic order.
2. The recorded relation of Christ to nature is clear. Blighting the fig tree, calming the storm, feeding the multitudes, walking on the water, casting out demons demonstrates His power over them.

HIS RELATION TO MANKIND
1. Jesus accepted the title of Messiah, Christ, Matt. 16:16, 17; Mark 14:61-62. He claimed to be the "Son of David," Mark 12:35-37. His favorite title was "Son of Man," relating Himself with the human family, and the Messianic hope.
2. While attached to men, He is apart from them:
    a. Jesus called all men unto Himself, setting Himself apart from the world of men, Matt. 11:28-30.
    b. He accepted the worship of men, Matt. 14:33; 28:17, while He taught that God only is the object of worship and service, Matt. 4:10.
    c. In prayer He saw Himself in a different relation to God from other men: it is "I," "me," "they," "them"; it is never "we," "us," etc.

HIS RELATION TO GOD
1. His unbroken fellowship with God, His God-consciousness, is an outstanding fact in the record. From the age of twelve at the earliest, his sense of

God's Fatherhood appears. It is one of the supreme notes of His doctrine, Luke 2:48, 49.
2. He claimed to reveal the Father, Matt. 11:27; John 7:29; 10:30; 14:7-9.
3. He never denied, but admitted equality with the Father, Matt. 26:63-66.
4. He declared His own omnipresence, Matt. 18:20; 28:20, and His omnipotence, Matt. 28:18-20.

CONCLUSION: APPLICATION OF THE ARGUMENT

Nothing is more obvious than the very commonplace axiom, that every *Effect* requires an adequate *Cause*.

"How did the evangelists solve this mighty problem of humanity with such perfect originality and precision? Only two answers are rationally possible: 1. They had before them the personal and historical Christ. 2. They wrote by inspiration of the Spirit of God. It cannot be otherwise" (Morehead, *op. cit.,* p. 55).

Refeeerences"

L. Boettner, *Studies in Theology,* p. 140-269.

Floyd Hamilton, *The Basis of Christian Faith,* p. 115-131. W.G. Morehead, *The Fundamentals,* Vol. III. pp. 42-60.

E.Y. Mullins, *Why Is Christianity True?,* p. 93-111.

B. Ramm, Protestant Christian Evidences, p. 163-183.

Lesson 19
Jesus Christ — The Method and Fullness of His Teaching

This lesson and the one to follow are, in reality, only continuations of the "Moral Glory" of Christ. Jesus Christ stands before us as the great Miracle of the ages. Jesus claims to be the "light of the world" (John 8:12). If one asks "is it true?" the reply is, "look around you and behold!" One writer declares, "He is the moral and spiritual Illuminator at this present moment of all the progressive nations on earth; and all who are not walking in His light are fallen into a state of stagnation and decay" (C.A. Row, *A Manual of Christian Evidences,* p. 29).

The whole of Christianity rests, not upon a philosophy or body of dogmas, but upon a Divine person, the Christ Himself. Jesus assigned to the moral evidences of His divine mission the first place in point of importance, and to what are commonly designated His miracles the second place. See John 8:18; 14:10, 11; Matt. 12:38-40, etc. In these lessons we are considering characteristics and peculiarities of Jesus which set Him apart from other men, convincing us that He is the Christ, the Son of God in an extraordinary sense. In this lesson we consider His peculiarities as a teacher which differentiate Him from men. (See Haygood's *Man of Galilee.*)

JESUS' METHOD OF THOUGHT DIFFERENCES HIM FROM MEN
1. Jesus does not seek the same end that the great thinkers have sought:
    a. *The Philosopher* seeks to explain the universe and its workings, to formulate a complete, all-embracing, all-explaining law of things. He studies the mind, seeking to explain it. He

Internal Evidences of Christianity 88

      speculates about evolution as an answer to the origin of things.
- b. *The Scientist* talks of atoms; the ontologist, of germs; the geologist, of rocks and formations, millions of years and various theoretical ages.
- c. *The Theologian* seeks a philosophy of religion, strives to show the origin of evil, advances theories of the atonement and such and is constantly seeking mysteries to explain.

2. Jesus is utterly different from these; He thinks in another realm.
   - a. Jesus raises no questions, seeks no explanations of things. To Him there is no mystery, nor need for an all-embracing formula and explanation of things.
   - b. Jesus did not philosophize about or try to explain God, although He claimed to know all about Him. He philosophized about nothing; He taught morals based upon truth. He taught truth itself.
   - c. Jesus never investigates; He never doubted His knowledge or questioned for a moment His ground or position. He did not "think to know," He knew. He knew all things.

JESUS' METHOD OF TEACHING DIFFERENCES HIM FROM MEN. "NEVER MAN SO SPAKE."

1. Jesus did not seek to prove things to His hearers, but announced His principles as truth, as God would announce truth. He did not reason to prove, or seek to discover; He simply taught truth as truth. Illustrations:
   - a. Of Providence and the Folly of Worry. In teaching His disciples of God's providence and the folly of worry, Jesus made no argument to prove His point, but used illustrations to impress

it: "lilies," "sparrows," Matt. 6:26-34.
- b. Of Prayer. Jesus made no argument about the nature of prayer, nor effort to prove its reasonableness or harmony with law; He simply taught the disciples to pray, Matt. 7:7-11; Luke 18:1, etc.
- c. Regarding the Sabbath. When Pharisees complained that He healed on that day, He asked them about their kindness to animals and the comparative values of a man and a sheep! Matt. 12:9-12.
- d. Of Religion. Jesus Christ, by one single utterance, has laid deep forever the religion of humanity, John 4 21-24. He settled the question of empty formality by teaching hardened ones of the Fatherhood of God, Luke 15.
2. Jesus never burdened His hearers with large words, philosophical reasonings, or the like, but spake simply, Mark 12:37.
3. Jesus possessed a divine calmness unseen in mere human teachers. He was always tenderhearted, compassionate, calm; he never became heated or excited in His discourses. He sought calmly to lead men out of darkness into light.

THE FULLNESS OF HIS TEACHING
DIFFERENCES JESUS FROM ALL MEN

1. Jesus taught as one having authority; He appealed not to the "rabbis," but to Moses, to the Prophets and to the Psalms: With these He was thoroughly familiar. He could speak with authority because: a. He knew His subject; He knew what He was talking about. He was an expert on the subject He handled. He never allowed Himself to be drawn away from it. b. He knew men. He knew the hearts of men; He knew the needs of men (John 2:2425). There was no

guesswork on His part.
2. He knew God. He walked with God; He lived with God; He prayed to God. There was nothing superficial in this knowledge, it was practical.
3. Jesus' teaching was a "full" teaching. Other teachers give principles of ethics and morals, but do they, any one of them, give a complete and full teaching as did Jesus? What moral principle has been added to the Sermon on the Mount? or have the centuries added to the work of the Christ?
4. The teaching of Jesus has more power upon the conscience than that exerted by any other teacher of any age. The words of men who knew not Jesus which exert the greatest influence on men, are those nearest like His own words. The teaching of those antagonistic to Jesus have no power over the conscience except to paralyze it.
5. Jesus lived what He taught; His teaching is explained by His life. a. Compare the teaching of the Sermon on the Mount with His life. b. In Him can no fault be found; nor can there be consciousness of fault or sin detected.
6. He claimed kinship with God, and that all things were delivered unto Him of God, but this does not shock us. We conclude He is "one with God."

CONCLUSION:
As all the colors combined make the pure white light, so the subjects of His teaching combine to make the sum total of all moral truth. Put the teachings of men together, all of them, and some shade will be wanting. The light will not be pure.

References:
A.G. Haygood, *The Man of Galilee*.
James Orr, *The Faith of a Modern Christian*, p. 101-118.

Lesson 20
Jesus Christ — The End He Proposed

Jesus Christ stands in a class by Himself. It was impossible for the Evangelists to have invented Him; hence, He lived as a historical character. His "moral glory" sets Him apart from men; His method of teaching, and the fullness of His teaching, difference Him from the common stock of humanity. These evidences all add together to convince us that Jesus is divine, the Christ of God.

The proposition of this particular lesson is, "The Magnitude of the End Jesus Proposed and Set About to Accomplish Proves Him Divine."

JESUS' ATTITUDE TOWARD SIN AND THE CIRCUMSTANCES OF MEN DIFFERENCE HIM FROM MEN.

1. Jesus saw in sin the root of all the ills of man, and the one thing to be remedied. This is peculiar to Him and His teaching. He recognized His mission to be one of saving men from sin, John 3:17, 18; 8:31-36; Luke 19:10. There was never a doubt at this point, John 12:32, 33.
2. Jesus' method of remedying the evil is also peculiar to Himself. He does not seek to change the circumstances of men, but to deliver men from Sin. He makes deliverance from sin the one thing needful. From His baptism and the beatitudes to the cross, His teaching is that man's need is salvation. Matt. 3:13-17; 5:1-10; 20:28; 26:28, etc.
3. His concern is for character, this likewise is peculiar to Himself. The gods of mythology always act to alter circumstances; Jesus acts to change the hearts of individuals. The heart is the seat of character and must be changed, Matt. 15:19-20; Luke 12:13-20; Matt. 5:8; 12:33-37.

Internal Evidences of Christianity   92

4. Jesus looked to bettering men, not conditions; with Him character is the test and measure of a man. This the Jews could not understand, so rejected and crucified Him. He proposed and sought to change the hearts of all men.

THE CONQUEST OF JESUS WAS WORLD-WIDE, FOR ALL TIME; NOT LOCAL OR TEMPORARY.

1. His undertaking was the spiritual re-creation of the human family, the entire world, John 10:16; Matt. 28:18-20; Mark 16:15-16; Luke 24:44-49.
2. He saw clearly the enormity of sin; He perceived perfectly the magnitude of His task, yet approached it with a calm dignity and assurance, John 12:32. Recognizing the heart as the seat of trouble, He declared that men *must be* born again, John 3:3-6.

THE PLANNING OF JESUS FOR THE ACCOMPLISHMENT OF SUCH A TASK WAS WHOLLY DIFFERENT FROM THE PLANS OF MEN. HE REPUDIATED THE METHODS OF MEN.

1. Jesus utterly excludes mere force. His symbol is not a sword but a cross, Matt. 26:5152. He rebuked the disciples for suggesting force, Luke 9:51-56. It was love He sought, and love dies under force.
2. Jesus did not use money to accomplish His end; man and Satan may bribe; Jesus repudiates and condemns such methods. When wealth is used for selfish ends, its possessor is a "fool," Luke 12:13-22.
3. Jesus excluded "diplomacy" from His method, which is the art of playing one selfishness against another. Truth must conquer, John 8:31-32; 17:17.
4. Jesus never appealed to selfish interests, but demanded complete surrender to Himself, Matt. 16:21-26.
    a. The disciples should have what is good for

them, Matt. 6:33, but even this should include "persecutions," Mark 10:30.
   b. Jesus could promise them no more in this world than He Himself had possessed, Matt. 8:18-20; John 13:16; 15:18-20.
5. Jesus did not do the things men do. He left no formal creed; He wrote no book; He founded no school; He did not even establish the church in His personal ministry; it is the outgrowth of His death and teaching.

JESUS TAUGHT OF A KINGDOM THAT SHOULD NEVER PERISH, BUT TOOK THE WAY OF PERISHING TO ESTABLISH AND PERPETUATE IT.

1. Here again Jesus was different from men. Many times He spoke of dying but never of a successor to take His place. Men should be told about HIM, believe on and obey HIM (Matt. 28:18-20); in this message the Kingdom should live.
2. He did not hide from the disciples the perils that should follow them.
3. The hand of the world was against Him: Jews, Romans, Greeks!

CONCLUSION:

Consider all this: Such an end! Such a plan! Such a promise! If Jesus were merely a man, this were lunacy!! But the centuries have given the answer.

References:

A.G. Haygood, The Man of Galilee

Lesson 21
Jesus Christ — and Miracles

Miracles are a definite part of Biblical teaching in both Old and New Testaments. They are inextricably interwoven into God's revelation of Himself. As the word of God, the Bible stands or falls at this very point. Either miracles occurred as actual happenings as recorded in the Bible, and the Bible is the word of God, or they did not occur and it is not the word of God, a special and divine revelation. The question will not down, it is always here. There can be no compromise in the matter.

DEFINITION OF "MIRACLE"
1. Three terms used: "In the New Testament, three terms are used to denote miracles. They are called "wonders," primarily in reference to the astonishment which they produce; "powers," as related to the divine energy to which they are due; and "signs," or tokens of God's presence and of the sanction thus afforded to the teacher or to what is taught." – George Park Fisher, *Manual of Christian Evidence,* p. 10. cf. J. Wendland, *Miracles and Christianity,* p. 7; R. Trench, *Notes on the Miracles,* p. 1-6.
2. Definition of "miracle":
    a. Faulkner: "A miracle is any deed in an order which is impossible to the forces ordinarily working in that order. Crystallization – at least perfect crystallization – is not a miracle in quartz; but it is a miracle in sandstone. Vegetable life is a miracle in minerals, but not in its own order, except in the sense in which all life is miracle. Animal life is a miracle to both. There are no forces in lower realm which can produce the higher, therefore these events are to

Internal Evidences of Christianity 96

      that lower order miracles." John Alfred Faulkner, *Modernism and the Christian Faith,* p. 59.

   b. Orr: "It may suffice here to define miracle as any deviation from or transcendence of the order of nature, due to the interposition of a supernatural cause." James Orr, *The Faith of a Modern Christian,* p. 65.

   c. Bettex: "What then is the Miracle? It is something which we do not understand because it does not conform to our ideas and our experience, nor does it coincide with the fragments of knowledge which we have obtained of the universe; in short, it is something inexplicable, whether we take it as the effect of laws not yet known, or as the direct intervention of an almighty God." F. Bettex, *The Miracle,* p. 13.

   d. "In agreement with Machen we assert that a miracle is an act of creation. It is a given, transcendent, supernatural act of God's power." Bernard Ramm, *Protestant Christian Evidences,* p. 128.

   e. An Explained Miracle: "An explained miracle is nonsense. Believe them or do not believe them – one only is possible... And if we believe these miracles, we may learn something about the miraculous from them." – Bettex, *op. cit.,* p. 72.

3. A miracle must be a sensible event, presented to the eye or ear. (Ramm)
4. Miracles must be seen within their Christian context. They are not isolated or unrelated.

SCIENCE AND MIRACLES

1. "Science treats of things that can be know; the miracle, on the other hand, according to its name

and nature, is that which is inexplicable and cannot be known. Therefore science and the miracle have nothing in common with each other. A miracle scientifically explained is a contradiction." Bettex, *op. cit.,* p. 33. "The great physicist Tyndal, though a skeptic, says: 'If there is a God, it is plain that He can perform miracles. Science however has not to treat of the miracle; because, if it exists, it lies without her sphere' (Fragments, New Edition)." *Ibid.,* p. 34.
2. "True, science shows us more and more that the universe is governed by fixed laws and that no manifestation is without its law; but in this she coincides with true religion. Even the most simple Christian, who, without much education and reasoning, considers the miracle a direct act of the Deity, believes, according to his Bible, that every act and thought of this God is Law." *Ibid.,* p. 37.
3. "But we learn more and more that these "triumphs of science' have no moral value." Trains, planes, radio, etc., p. 39. "Because modern science is forgetful of the soul and treats almost exclusively of the body, we are gradually sinking into a mechanical and materialistic view of the world, the worship of the machine, of techniques, and the utilization of matter. The fear of "blind natural forces' is taking hold of us, the cult of the atom, pale apprehension of the baccilus. We fear the infinitely small because we no longer revere the infinitely great. Faith in a wonderful God and in His miracles cannot thrive in such soil." *Ibid.,* p. 57.

MIRACLES AND REVELATION
1. Miracles are possible.
    a. MacCartney: "When you face this question of miracles, it all depends upon what kind of a God

Internal Evidences of Christianity 98

you believe in, and whether or not you spell His name with a capital "G." C.E. MacCartney, *Christian faith and the Spirit of the Age,* p. 70, 71.
   b. Bettex: To deny miracles is equivalent to the assertion, "We, who have dwelt upon this earth only since yesterday already know all laws, all forces, all possibilities of the universe... human knowledge will never be competent to decide what is possible. The possibility of miracles is therefore established." *op. cit.,* pp. 13, 14.
2. Miracles are probable.
   a. Admit God and miracles become possible. Acknowledge sin, and the intervention of God. on man's behalf becomes probable, and upon the probability of God's intervention on man's behalf rests the probability miracle; for miracle and redemption by revelation go hand in hand.
   b. Orr: "Do the difficulties attaching to the idea of miracle, or to its proof, justify us in rejecting the miracles pertaining to the Biblical revelation?" *op. cit.,* p. 72.
   c. Fisher: "The anterior probability that a revelation will be given lies in the necessitous condition of man and the benevolent character of *God."* *op. cit.,* p. 22.

   The need of revelation is then suggested by Prof. Fisher under four points: a. "The first is the vagueness and uncertainty of man's knowledge, under the light of nature, of God and divine things." pp. 22, 23. b. "There is a sense of guilt which reveals itself in the rites of the religions of the heathen nations. It is the consciousness of being unreconciled to the Power on whom we depend and to whom a more or less distinct feeling of responsibility prevails among mankind." p. 24.

"There is a bondage of habit which often gives rise to an ineffectual struggle and to a craving for supernatural help." p. 24. b. "There is the need, under the sufferings of life, of sources of strength, such as the light of nature does not afford. Relief under afflictions, peace in sorrow, salvation from despondency, are wants which are deeply felt." p. 24. All of these needs Christianity meets.

3. Christianity originates in and with Jesus; and Jesus is definitely associated with miracles. Evidence that miracles were wrought by Jesus:
   a. Fisher: (1) "On different occasions Jesus is said to have told those whom He miraculously healed not to make it publicly known (Matt. 9:30:12:16; 17:9; Mark 3:12; Luke 5:14; 8:56; etc.). He wished to avoid a public excitement having little or no kinship with moral and spiritual feeling." pp. 37, 38. (2) "Cautions, which are plainly authentic, against an excessive esteem of miracles, are said to have been uttered by Jesus (John 4:48; 14:11; Matt. 16:3; Luke 10:17). No one who made up stories of miracles would connect with his accounts a disparagement of them, or anything that looked like it (see also Luke 10:20)." p. 38. (3) "There are sayings of Christ ... which are inseparable from the miracles with which they are connected (see Matt. 11: 4; Luke 14:5; 17:22)." p. 38.
   b. MacCartney: "The Miracles and the Gospel stand or fall together... not only is the unity of Christ's personality broken if we reject the miracles – for history knows but one Christ, the

Internal Evidences of Christianity 100

   Christ of the Gospels and that Christ worked miracles – but the integrity of Christ is destroyed." *op. cit.,* pp. 77,78.
   c. Fisher: "The evangelists ascribe to Jesus no miracles prior to His baptism. Cf. with apocryphal gospels." p. 40. "Moreover, no miracles are attributed to John the Baptist, notwithstanding that so much value is attached in the Gospels to his testimony to Jesus. If there had been a disposition to make up stories of miracles that did not occur, why is not John credited with works of a like nature?" p. 40.
4. Purpose of Miracles:
   a. "Miracles are aids to faith. They come in with decisive effect to convince those who are impressed by the moral evidence that they are not deceived, and that God is in reality speaking through men. According to the New Testament histories it was in this light that miracles were regarded by Jesus. Where there was no spiritual preparation, no dawning faith, He refused to perform miracles." p. 19. Fisher, *op. cit.*
   b. MacCartney: "The purpose of the miracles is stated in the sentence spoken by Jesus when he summoned Lazarus to come forth from the grave, 'That they may know that thou hast sent me.'" p. 80. See Matt. 9:9; John 11:42; 20:30,31.

References:

F. Bettex, *The Miracle,* (the entire book is good).
Lorraine Boettner, *Studies in Theology,* pp. 176-179.
G.W. Everest, *The Divine Demonstration,* pp. 22-28. 241-248.
Clarence MacCartney, *Christian Faith and the Spirit of the Age*, pp. 68-80.
James Orr, *The Faith of a Modern Christian*, pp. 61-80.

Bernard Ramm, *Protestant Christian Evidences*, pp. 155-162.

C. Trench, *Notes on the Miracles*.

Lesson 22
Miracles and Their Moral Relationship

With the possibility and probability of miracles established, it now remains to be seen whether there is a relation between the physical miracles of Jesus and the moral nature of His kingdom -If this can be established, then the probability becomes stronger.

The Gospel of John is not a biography of Christ's life, but a few selected events of a few of the days of His ministry. Of the more than one thousand days of His personal ministry, John selects events out of only twenty at the most. More than one third (by verses) of the book is devoted to the last twenty-four hours of His life.

The Gospel according to John presents the conflict between Jesus and Satan, in which the conflict mounts in intensity until it looks as if Satan has triumphed. But not so! Christ is raised from the dead and light and truth triumph. The victory is complete. Jesus is proved to be the Son of God.

The Gospel of John is probably the strongest book in the New Testament as evidence to the deity of Jesus. Christ's deity combined with His humanity is John's theme. The purpose of his writing is summarized in John 20:30-31. The theme of this lesson is the moral quality of the signs as evidence to His deity. Each has a moral significance. Each tends to relate Jesus to the moral and physical universe – He is Lord of all.

THE "I AM'S" OF JESUS

Eternal existence of Jesus is claimed by Himself as He said, "Before Abraham was born, I am," John 8:58. Cf. with Exodus 3:13, 14. That He is the Christ is confessed by Himself to the woman of Samaria, 4:26; The signs presented confirm both His eternal "I am" and His Messiahship.

1. Bread of life, 6:35.
2. Light of the world, 8:12.
3. Door of entrance to pasture and protection, 10:7-9.
4. The good shepherd, 10:11, 14.
5. Way, truth, life, 14:6.
6. Vine through whom is supplied all succor, 15:1-8.
7. Resurrection and the life, 11:25-

II. THE SIGNS WHICH CONFIRM THE CLAIMS, AND THEIR MORAL QUALITIES

1. Water to wine, 2:1-11. A social Being; the "All-provident one" who provided only the best. He is proved to be the Master of matter, of substances, and of creation.
2. Healing of the nobleman's son, 4:46-54. Demonstrating power over distance, with Him it is no factor; and power over disease: "I am the life."
3. Lame man at Bethesda, 5:1-18. Master of time, thirty-eight years no factor, power over ills, He came from God, can do only as He sees the Father doing, 5:19.
4. Feeding of the five thousand; loaves and fishes, ch. 6. "I am the bread of life."
5. Walking on the water, 6:16-21. The door to safety; the way. Sight to the blind, ch. 9. The light; the provider of light.
6. Raising of Lazarus, ch. 11. The resurrection and the life.

CONCLUSION:

None of us has ever seen a miracle. But as one beholds Jesus in the midst of a moral world, as one sees His works, all of which have a moral significance, He Himself becomes the miracle of the age. As one beholds Him: His claims, His works, His power over the heart, one asks for no greater miracle than Jesus.

With the possibility and probability of miracles established and with the work and life of Jesus welded inseparably together with them – if the resurrection can be proved, which is the supreme miracle, all other miracles stand verified; if it cannot, they do not matter.

References:
Merrill Tenney, *John, The Gospel of Belief.*

PART FIVE – THE RESURRECTION

Lesson 23
"If Christ Be Not Raised"

The importance of the resurrection of Jesus from the dead is suggested by the fact that it is mentioned directly one hundred four or more times in the New Testament (R.A. Torrey, *Fundamentals,* Vol. V., p. 81).

The resurrection of the body of Jesus Christ, the very foundation rock of the Christian religion, is questioned today by many so-called scholars in the field of religion. Some of the present theories are: There was a resurrection of spirit (which was never buried), the resurrection of His cause (which likewise was not buried, but which was just being born), etc.

E.Y. Mullins has well expressed the whole issue when he said, "By resurrection it is meant that the body of Jesus was changed from a dead to a living body. What was laid in the grave dead came forth therefrom alive. This and nothing less is the Christian claim" *(Why Is Christianity True?* pp. 188, 9). R.A. Torrey has aptly said, "while the literal bodily resurrection of Jesus Christ is the corner-stone of the Christian doctrine, it is also the Gibraltar of Christian Evidence, and the Waterloo of infidelity and rationalism" *(Fundamentals,* V., p. 82).

This lesson relates itself with the points of salvation involved in the resurrection. "IF CHRIST HATH NOT BEEN RAISED" (I Cor. 15:12-19).

"THEN IS OUR PREACHING VAIN"
1. From the first sermon the Apostles had testified to the great fact of the resurrection of Jesus from the dead, Acts 2:24, 32; 3:13-15; 4:33; 17:30, 31.
2. If the Apostles cannot be believed at this point, how can they be believed at any point? Away goes faith even in a "historical Jesus," and hope topples to earth, for faith is the under-support of hope, Heb.

11:1.
3. If the Apostles are to be believed at this point, then they must be believed in all things they taught, and if believed, then Christ must be obeyed, for He is Lord and Christ, Acts 2:36.

"WE ARE FOUND FALSE WITNESSES OF GOD"
1. Their testimony had been that God raised Jesus. This had been their testimony from the beginning.
2. This was to have been their mission as apostles, John 15:27.
3. Their selection as apostles required that they be able to bear this witness, Acts 1:21, 22.
4. John testifies that they were qualified by three senses: ear, eye, touch, I John 1:1.

"YOUR FAITH IS VAIN"
1. The religion of Christ is a religion of faith, Rom. 5:1, 2; I Cor. 5:7. But FAITH relies upon TESTIMONY, and testimony to FACTS. The fundamental fact of Christian faith is the resurrection of Christ. If not raised, then our faith is vain, for there is no fact believed, but only falsehood.
2. Faith that saves is faith in the Christ whom God raised, not faith in merely a good man. John 8:24.
3. Christ's claims are a hollow mockery if no resurrection, for He claimed to be the Christ and that the sign of Jonah should be the proof of his claim. Matt. 12:38-40.

"YE ARE YET IN YOUR SINS"
1. The blood was shed for remission of sins, Matt. 26:28; but it was presented by Christ as the high priest, Heb. 9:11-14; 10:19-22.
2. As High Priest, He was made such after the power of an endless life, Heb. 7:16; "He ever liveth," Heb.

7:25; He was "appointed a son perfected for ever more," Heb. 7:28.

3. Hence, if not raised from the dead, He is no High Priest, and the blood is of no avail, "ye are yet in your sins."

"THEN THEY ALSO THAT ARE FALLEN ASLEEP IN CHRIST HAVE PERISHED."

1. If not raised, then man is without hope, for all hope rests upon the resurrection of Jesus from the dead, Heb. 11:1; I Peter 1:20, 21.
2. The resurrection of Jesus is proof of immortality, Luke 20:37, 38. This cannot be believed if no resurrection; by the gospel it was brought to light, 2 Tim. 1:10.
3. Hope of our resurrection, of heaven, of God, rests upon Jesus' resurrection.

CONCLUSION:

The whole superstructure of the Christian's salvation and hope rests on the resurrection of Jesus from the dead. If evidence is sufficient to prove this fact, then faith follows; if not, the whole system collapses.

Lesson 24
His Resurrection — The Witnesses

"But now hath Christ been raised from the dead, the first-fruits of them that are asleep," is the triumphant cry of the Apostle Paul (I Cor. 15:20). This proposition is the keystone of the Christian's faith. It is the support of his every hope. There is little use to argue about the rest of the miracles of the New Testament: if Christ be raised from the dead, the rest of the miracles are easy to accept; if He be not risen, the rest do not matter.

If the resurrection of Jesus Christ can be proved as a fact in history, then He is the Christ of God and the Bible is a special divine revelation. We believe the testimony is such that it is more reasonable to believe than not to believe.

THE QUESTION AND THE WITNESSES
1. The Question: Did Jesus rise from the dead?

"By the leading skeptics it is now admitted, first, that Jesus actually died and was buried; second, it is admitted that on or before the third morning His body disappeared from the tomb; third, that the disciples came to believe firmly that He arose from the dead. The exact issue has reference to the last two facts, and may be stated by the two questions: Did the body disappear by a resurrection, or in some other way? and Did the belief of the disciples originate from the fact of the resurrection, or from some other cause?" (J.W. McGarvey, *Evidences of Christianity*, Part III, pp. 117, 118).

2. The Witnesses:

"To us the witnesses are a group of women, not less than five in number; the twelve older apostles; and the apostle Paul. The testimony of the women and the twelve is recorded in the four Gospels, in Acts, and in the Epistles of Peter and John, and in Revelation. That of Paul is found in

Acts and his epistles." *(Ibid.* p. 118).

THE APOSTLES AS WITNESSES TO THE RESURRECTION

"The force of human testimony depends on three things: first, the honesty of the witnesses; second, their competency; and third, their number" (J.W. McGarvey, *op. cit.,* p. 146).

1. Their honesty. "We ascertain whether they are honest by considering their general character and their motives in the particular case" *(Ibid.).* Judged by all the testimony available, their character is good.
   a. Their tone. They tell their story in the dispassionate tone that belongs to truthful witnesses.
   b. Their candor in relating things to their own discredit. They show their honesty in relating things discreditable to themselves: Peter's denial, the Apostles' ambition, their failure to understand, etc.
   c. Their sufferings. The sincerity and honesty of the Apostles is proved by what they were willing to endure in consequence of the testimony they gave. They had no selfish advantage to gain.
   d. Allusions to local customs. The truthfulness of the witnesses is shown by many incidental (and, therefore, undesigned) allusions to the topography, customs, and manners of the country to peculiarities of time and place. These things confirm their credibility.
   e. The unintentional evidence of words, phrases, and accidental details: Jesus was not at first recognized by His disciples, Luke 24:16; John 21:4; but not told why. "Touch me not ... "(John

His Resurrection—The Witnesses

20:17); what is the meaning? "I will take him away" (John 20:15); could she? "And Peter "(Mark 16:7) Why? "The napkin" (John 20:7), an incidental thing. And a thousand other examples.

    f. Character of the interviews with Jesus. The character of these interviews of Jesus with His followers constitute unanswerable proof of the resurrection.

    g. Manifestations of Jesus. These were limited to a certain number of instances; all these interviews ceased after a limited, not very long time. No appearances to His enemies. All of this points to the honesty of these men as witnesses, b. "The motives which prompt men to false testimony are *fear, avarice,* and *ambition;* fear of some evil to themselves or others, which is to be averted by the testimony; desire of sordid gain; and ambition for some kind of distinction among men" (McGarvey, *Ibid.*)̧. In this they are above suspicion.

2. Their competency. "Competency is determined by considering the opportunities of the witness to obtain knowledge of that to which he testifies, and his mental capacity to observe and remember the facts" (McGarvey, *Ibid.*).

    a. Opportunity. The Apostles had been with Him from His baptism, and understood that their office was that of witnesses (Acts 1:21, 22).

    b. Mentally competent. Note the character and occupation of at least three: Matthew was a tax gatherer, with a profound knowledge of Hebrew law, Roman law, and human nature. He shows no sign of hysteria or weakness.

    c. Peter, although impetuous, was not credulous.

    d. Nor was John credulous. He shows an aptness at

noting details, (John 20:7).
   e. These men were not willing to believe just anything, Mk. 9:30-32; Lk. 24:25.
3. The number. "The requisite number varies with the degree of probability attached to the facts. The testimony of two honest and competent witnesses makes us feel more sure than of one; and that of three, than that of two; but a limit is soon reached beyond which those who are convinced feel the need of no more, and those who are not yet convinced realize that more would not convince them. When this number has testified in any case, the number is sufficient, and a greater number would be useless" (McGarvey, *Ibid.*).

THE EVIDENCE OF THE CHANGED DISCIPLES
1. Jesus repeatedly told His disciples He must be killed and raised from the dead on the third day, Mt. 12:38-40; 16:21; 17:9; 20:19; John 2:19.
2. This they did not understand, nor even believe after the resurrection, Lk. 24:11, 20-21; Mark 16:12-14. So complete was their feeling that all was over, even though they had seen Him, they returned to their old occupation of fishing, Jn. 21:3.
3. But after Jesus' ascension and the coming of the Holy Spirit,
4. behold the difference, Acts 2:14, 22-24, 36; 3:13-15; 4:8-13, 19-20; 5:28-32, etc.
5. How is this change to be accounted for? No man can deny the zeal of the Apostles, for their message took the world, changed history, overturned existing systems. Peter's explanation, I Peter 1:3-5.

CONCLUSION:
It is easier to believe Peter's explanation than to believe the explanations given by men in an effort to account for Jesus Christ and His influence.

His Resurrection—The Witnesses

References for this and the following lessons:

A. Alexander, *Evidences of Christianity*, pp. 118-130.
Bond, *Positive Christian Evidences*, pp. 231-253.
W.A. Candler, *Christus Auctor,* see table of contents.
Fisher, *Manual of Christian Evidences*, pp. 44ff., 83ff.
Floyd Hamilton, *Basis of Christian Faith,* pp. 283-295.
I.S. B. E., Article, "Resurrection."
McClintock and Strong Encyclopedia, article, "Resurrection of Jesus Christ."
J.W. McGarvey, *Evidences of Christianity,* pp. 116ff, 132-162, 163ff.
E.Y. Mullins, *Why Is Christianity True?*, pp. 185-203.
James Orr, *Christian View of God and the World*, 478 (See Index, "Resurrection").
James Orr, *The Resurrection of Jesus.*
William Ramsey, *The Resurrection of Christ.*
Edward J. Carnell, *Introduction to Christian Apologetics,* pp. 243-275, 336-348.
Merrill Tenney, *John, The Gospel of Belief,* pp. 272-284.
Wilbur Smith, *Therefore Stand,* pp. 359-437.
Russell, *A Lawyer's Examination of the Bible*, pp. 101-136.

Lesson 25
The Empty Tomb

The purpose for which John wrote is summarized by himself in these words, "That ye may believe that Jesus is the Christ, the Son of God; and that believing ye may have life in His name" (20:30-31).

One-third of the book (by verses) is devoted to the last twenty-four hours of His life. The object of the whole is Belief. In the cross, unbelief and belief reach their climax. In the resurrection His claim to deity is verified and His victory is complete.

THE CRUCIFIXION (Gospel of John)
1. The trial: Pilate's opportunity, and his rejection of truth, 18:28-19:16.
2. In presenting the actual act of crucifixion, John omits the revolting details. No stress is laid on the physical suffering.
3. The title by Pilate, 19:17-22. Two-fold significance:
    a. Pilate's hatred and contempt for the Jews; and an ironic statement of truth.
4. Fulfilled scriptures, evidence of His deity:
    a. Scriptures pertaining to the Cross.
        i. The entry into Jerusalem, 12:12-16; Zech. 9:9-10.
        ii. The rejection by the Jews, 12:36-43; Isa. 53; and their hatred for Him, John 15:25; Ps. 35:19; 69:4.
        iii. The betrayal by Judas, John 13:18; 17:12; Ps. 41:9.
    b. On the Cross
        i. The parting of His garments, 19:24; Ps. 22:18.
        ii. Vinegar in His thirst, 19:28; Ps. 69:21.
        iii. Not a bone broken, though the side was

pierced, 19:32-37; Ex. 12:46; Num. 9:12; Ps. 34:20; Zech. 12:10.
5. The finished purpose, evidence of His deity: sacrifice for sins, 1:29; 3:14; 10:11, 15-17; 12:24, 32-33. Now finished! A cry of triumph, 19:30.
6. Certainty of His death: testimony of the bowed head, of the soldiers, and of Nicodemus and Joseph of Aramathaea.
7. It looks as if the darkness has triumphed; as if Satan has won.

THE RESURRECTION – THE EVIDENCE OF THE EMPTY TOMB
1. The open door, the stone rolled away, 20:1-2.
   a. Rolled away by friends or by enemies?
   b. Why opened, to let Jesus out or to let the disciples in?
2. Peter and John: grave cloths, napkin, John believed, 20:3-10. Personal appearances of Jesus:
   a. To Mary, "Touch me not," go tell the brethren, 20:11-18.
   b. To disciples, "Peace," 20:19-24.
   c. To Thomas, the pessimist, "Be not faithless, but believing," 20:26, 27.

EFFECT OF THE RESURRECTION
1. On Mary: from a frustrated woman to a bringer of good news.
2. Peter: Ran to the tomb. Concern for Jesus? or for forgiveness?
3. John: keen observer, "Believed."
4. Disciples' from fearful men to bold, courageous witnesses.
5. Thomas: the climax of evidence. From a skeptic to strongest of belief: "My Lord and my God." and this from a Jew! Possibly John's greatest human witness to the resurrection.

CONCLUSION:

The conflict between belief and unbelief has been presented. The triumph of truth is absolute. The evidence is sufficiently conclusive to convince any honest individual that Jesus was raised from the dead; therefore, He is the Christ of God.

Lesson 26
The Witness of Monuments

As in nature where "God has not left Himself without witness" to His creative acts and providence (Acts 14:17), so in the spiritual realm He has not left Himself without monuments to the Divine origin of Christianity. Since the resurrection of Jesus is the fundamental fact and foundation of the whole system, God has provided ample evidence in proof of the fact. The institutions of Christianity bear witness as monuments to the resurrection of Jesus Christ from the dead.

The evidence of these we consider in this lesson.

THE CHURCH
1. The church is here, and has been for nineteen centuries. It rests upon the deity of Christ, which deity is proved by the resurrection, Matt. 12:38-40; 16:13-20; Rom. 1:3-4; I Cor. 3:10, 11; 15:17.
2. That this should be its foundation was foretold in prophecy, Isa. 28:16; Psalm 118:22-24.
3. Beginning with three thousand, and soon filling the civilized world, the church was despised, persecuted, hated and fought on every hand, yet it rested on one support: the resurrection of Jesus Christ.

THE BIBLE
1. The Book is here, all admit that. The order: CHRIST—CHURCH—BOOK.
2. The Book is a product of the church, which is a product of the resurrection. What is in the Book is in it, which is either fact or fiction. If fact, Christ was raised; if fiction, as great a miracle was performed in creating its character and teaching, and pawning them on the world, as in creating the

world. It is in the world today a monument to the resurrection of Christ.

THE LORD'S DAY
1. How far back has it been a special day of worship? Only from Pentecost. Jews observed the seventh day, Gentiles various days; both, united in Christ, observed the first day, the day of the resurrection.
2. It has stood from the beginning a monument to the resurrection, Acts 20:7; Rev. 1:10.

THE LORD'S SUPPER
1. Here is another institution observed by Christians from the beginning, Acts 2:42.
2. Though commemorative of His death, it is indirectly commemorative of the resurrection, for it is to be "till He come," I Cor. 11:26. This affirms the resurrection; He cannot come if not raised.

NEW SIGNIFICANCE OF BAPTISM
1. John's work was preparatory to the coming of Christ (Isa. 40:3-5). This baptism was for remission of sins, Mark 1:1-5.
2. But from Pentecost a new significance was attached to baptism; it was into the death of Christ and a resurrection with Him, Romans 6:3-5; Col. 2:12.
3. It was the evidence of the resurrection that moved three thousand to be baptized, Acts 2:41.

CONCLUSION:
The monuments all testify to the resurrection of Jesus. They stand and have stood for nineteen hundred years.

Lesson 27
Proof From the Conversion of Saul

This is an outline of the argument made by Lord George Lyttelton, which first appeared about 1747. Lyttelton and his friend, Gilbert West, were "Fully persuaded that the Bible was an impostor and determined to expose the cheat. Lord Lyttelton chose the conversion of Paul and Mr. West the Resurrection of Christ for the subject of hostile criticism... the result of their separate attempts was, that they were both converted by their efforts to overthrow the truth of Christianity." *(The Fundamentals,* Vol. V., p. 107, Reprinted in *Evidence Quarterly,* 1:2, p. 9.)

Lyttelton lays down four propositions which he considers exhaust all the possibilities in the case:
1. Either Paul was "an imposter who said what he knew, to be false, with an intent to deceive"; or
2. He was an enthusiast who imposed on himself by the force of "an overheated imagination;" or
3. He was "deceived by the fraud of others;" or finally,
4. What he declared to be the cause of his conversion did all really happen; "and, therefore the Christian religion is a divine institution."

PAUL WAS NOT AN IMPOSTER
Men act from motive and there could have been no motive for imposture:
1. *Wealth* could not have been the motive; wealth was on the side of those forsaken, poverty on the side espoused. Even though poor and in want, he refused, to accept help when such would hinder the gospel, 1 Cor. 4:11-13; 2 Cor. 12:14; Acts 20:3 3-34. The closing picture of his life is that of an old man in a Roman prison, asking that a cloak be sent him to protect him from the cold, 2 Tim. 4:13.
2. *Reputation* was not the motive, for reputation lay on

the side of the Pharisees, universal contempt on the side chosen, I Cor. 1:26-29; 4:11-13.
3. *Power did not motivate him;* that is, the desire for power. He had no eye for worldly ambition when he became a Christian. He addressed his inferiors as "co-laborers," "fellow-workers;" he neither lorded it over individuals, nor over the churches he established. Paul preached Christ as head, hid himself behind the cross, and rebuked sin of all kind in the churches, without fear or favor, but never with an air of superiority, Philemon 23-24; I Cor. 1:13-17; 3:4-9; 2 Cor. 4:5.
4. *The gratification of fleshly passion* could not have been the motive. Some may claim revelations in order to indulge in loose conduct, but Paul preached the highest standard of morals, and condemned all departures from such a standard, Eph. 4:17-5:33; Col. 3:5-17; Gal. 5:19-25.
5. *Was it simply a pious fraud?* Did Paul pretend conversion simply to spread Christianity? Answer: We are back where we started, What was the motive? Men have some motive in what they do, what was Paul's? Where did he get his knowledge? How account for his success?

PAUL WAS NOT AN ENTHUSIAST WHO IMPOSED ON HIMSELF
1. Definition of enthusiast: "A religious—madman; a fanatic. One whose mind is wholly possessed and heated by what engages it... A fervent and imaginative person." Webster.
2. Elements of an Enthusiast.
    a. Great heat of temper. Though Paul was fervent, he was always governed by reason and discretion. Before all, his effort was to reach men with the gospel, Acts 24:24-27; 26:2-29.

Proof from the Conversion of Saul

   He had one aim only, Phil. 3:13, 14.
   b. Melancholy. This is a mark of misguided zeal, but it is never found in Paul; he is always rejoicing, never brooding, Col. 1:24; Phil. 4:4-7, etc.
   c. Paul was not swept away as an enthusiast, for such men always see what they are looking for; he was looking for anything else. He was persecuting Christ, not looking for Him.

PAUL WAS NOT DECEIVED BY OTHERS
1. Nor was he deceived by others, for such was a moral impossibility. While Paul was bitter against the disciples they could never have attempted such a feat as deceiving him in such a way – a moral impossibility.
2. It was physically impossible for them to have produced the light and the voice with which to deceive him.
3. THEREFORE, Paul saw Jesus Christ on the road to Damascus, Christ RAISED FROM THE DEAD.

TESTIMONY OF PAUL TO THE RESURRECTION
(Supplementary to the above by Candler)
1. Universal belief in the resurrection:
   a. Paul's unquestioned epistles: Romans, Galatians, 1 and 2 Corinthians.
   b. Claims in them: Romans 1:4; Gal. 1:1; I Cor. 15:14, 15.
2. Also, the resurrection was a matter of faith in those churches addressed, even the one Paul had not visited, i.e., Rome.
3. Paul met his opponents by an appeal to having seen Jesus, I Cor. 9:1. This establishes the fact that his opponents believed in the resurrection and that Paul's having seen Jesus was requisite to apostleship.

Internal Evidences of Christianity 126

4. Three theories by which to account for this universal belief:
   a. An intended fraud by the apostles.
   b. The apostles were deceived.
   c. Jesus was raised from the dead.
5. A consideration of these:
   a. The early disciples lacked motive and ability for a fraud so stupendous and successful. If not raised, we have here a wonderful effect without an adequate cause.
   b. "These men lacked the mental conditions required for such an hallucination as the 'vision theory' attributed to the early followers of Jesus. One of the three mental conditions must exist before the mind can yield itself to an hallucination, viz., prepossession, a fixed idea, or a state of expectancy." (Candler, *Christus Auctor,* p. 86).
   c. "Again, why should the same form of hallucination have possessed the minds of so many and so different persons at the same time?" *(Ibid.,* p. 87)
   d. "Furthermore, if the appearances of Jesus were mere visions, why did they cease within a very limited time after the crucifixion — say forty days? What cured the visionaries of their hallucinations all at once? Why were they all cured simultaneously? Why did not the distemper last them longer?" *(Ibid.,* p. 88)

CONCLUSION:
There is only one logical answer: Jesus Christ was raised from the dead; He is the Son of God; and The Bible is a Special Divine Revelation. The evidence sustains the proposition with which the study began. It is more rational to believe than to disbelieve.

www.ingramcontent.com/pod-product-compliance
Lightning Source LLC
Chambersburg PA
CBHW060839050426
42453CB00008B/750